Contents

Preface   iii

Acknowledgements   iv

1 You, the Teacher, As a Human Being   1

2 The Child Himself   6

3 The Child's Family and Home   12

4 Animals In and Out of the Classroom   19

5 Breaking Bread: Customs and Pleasures of Eating   32

6 Cooking: Sensory Involvement   42

7 Seeds and Plants; Flowers and Fruits   54

8 Transportation: Everything Goes   61

9 Safety: Awareness in Action   70

10 The Child as a Multimedia Artist   80

11 Water, Sand, and Other Natural Materials   97

12 Holidays, Celebrations, and Other Occasions   107

13 The Threshold of Literacy   121

14 Places to Go and People to Know   132

15 Striving for Concepts in Preschool Education   141

Bibliography   149

Index   152

FROM HAND TO HEAD

A Handbook for Teachers of Preschool Programs

MARGUERITA RUDOLPH

SCHOCKEN BOOKS · NEW YORK

First published by SCHOCKEN BOOKS 1977

Published by arrangement with McGraw-Hill Book Company
Copyright © 1973 by McGraw-Hill, Inc.

Library of Congress Cataloging in Publication Data

Rudolph, Marguerita.
  From hand to head.

  Bibliography: p.149
  Includes index.
  1. Education, Preschool. 2. Activity programs
  in education. I. Title.

[LB1140.R777 1977]   372.1'1'02   76-39624

Manufactured in the United States of America

Preface

Throughout the years of working with groups of preschool children and associating with parents and teachers, I have come to realize that early learning proceeds *from hand to head.* Learning from physical contacts and encounters, under congenial conditions, gradually reaches the workings of the mind, and with human influence results in the development of meaningful skills.

Young children need to have a hand, their own hand, in every activity while they are learning so that what they learn sticks to their growing ribs and becomes part of themselves as maturing persons. How can a teacher provide for and be able to manage and live with such activity? How can she assess young children's different strengths as well as recognize their many limitations? How can she judge their mental grasp? How can a teacher prepare and organize a classroom so that an atmosphere of freedom and a sense of love and order are maintained most of the time? To explore such questions and to search for some answers in real situations are the goals of this "hand" (and "head") book.

M. R.

Fresh Meadows, New York
November 1972

Acknowledgments

It is impossible to acknowledge all the helpful human sources which led me to the writing and rewriting of this book. Some sources are evident, but subtle sources are no less significant.

I prevailed upon a few people to read some chapters in the rough. Their interest and insight, their criticism and praise gave me substantial encouragement! Among those people are Barbara Biber, Distinguished Research Scholar, Bank Street College of Education; Lucille Lindberg, Professor of Education, Queens College; and Miss Jessie Stanton, indefatigable worker in many areas and institutions of Early Childhood Education.

While working in various schools and centers over the years, I gathered much material and stored it in mind, as well as in writing. Such material is a treasure, a great gift to a writer. Among the giving schools are Fresh Meadows Nursery School, where I was a teacher when Miss Margaret Fitchen was Director there; Great Neck Community School, where I worked the longest as Director; and, most recently, Queens College Early Childhood Center, which my grandchildren attended and where I worked as a substitute classroom teacher.

In the writing of this handbook I have been very much aware of my daughter Alicia Kaufmann, a teacher and a writer, and frequently took into account her educational concerns as well as her literary demands.

The most needed help of all, that in the scrupulous rewriting, came from a sensitive, yet questioning and practical, editor, Mrs. Virginia S. Brown.

To Bank Street College of Education with its many innovative and inspiring people, who have encouraged my learning and writing, I dedicate this handbook.

1 You, the Teacher, As a Human Being

You may be a teacher in a nursery school, in a kindergarten, in a day care center, in a Head Start class, in a preschool connected with a college or sponsored as a parent cooperative, or in still another kind of early childhood setting. There has been unprecedented growth in the number and types of preschool programs in the last five years. According to census figures *one of every five children* under five years of age was enrolled in a program in 1970, as compared to one of every ten children in 1965.[1] Although federally supported projects for children of poverty families have been responsible for most of the increase, programs for children on the other rungs of the economic ladder have also risen to meet social and educational needs of our youngest.

You are, therefore, in the category of teachers whose numbers are now rapidly increasing, whose value is becoming more and more recognized by educators on all levels and by members of many other professions, and whose prestige in the community and in the nation is rising. With the demand for services comes a higher scale of pay. Expansion of programs and financial security should not in themselves lead to contentment. You cannot pat

[1] Jack Rosenthal. "Nursery Schools Growing Rapidly." In *The New York Times*, Nov. 10, 1971.

yourself on the back and take your job for granted—though some teachers do. To have teaching be meaningful to you, you need to take stock and ask some questions: *Who* am I? *What* am I doing? *How* am I doing?

Your first asset as a preschool teacher is the kind of human being you are, which differs from your qualifications as a college graduate professionally trained and properly accredited. Your asset as a human being is also something other than the appropriately dressed, mannered, and well-spoken citizen. Your qualities as a human being are deeper than your official credentials or appearance, and they count for more in your effectiveness as a teacher.

One of your important human assets is your liking children enough to want to work in *their behalf*. This is a first priority and it is different from your loving children generally or enjoying them at times. It means caring about children's interests and needs more than about your own convenience or implementation of efficient plans.

Your asset as a human being is your ability to feel what a child's needs are and respond on the spot. At crucial times you must put yourself in the child's place—yet not remain there too long. This is not easy. It takes real struggle sometimes to have a handkerchief ready for a crying child and not stay there and cry with him or to keep watch on a child experiencing difficulty in climbing a ladder and keep hands off unless needed.

When you deal with children and their families, it is not easy to be a helping human adult, striving to be mature and to manage your own feelings of frustration and anger. You have to be a listener with an open mind and heart as well as ears.

How does one become such a human being? Maybe you were born that way. Maybe responsibilities at an early age helped you. Or, maybe you had special love and care while you were a child. Maybe you are like your mother or your father who influenced you or a teacher who guided you. Or, you may credit God with your human endowment. There is no known prescription for making a good human being. It cannot be guaranteed by any constitution or culture.

It may give you comfort to realize that as a human being, you, the preschool teacher, are never really alone. There are in your school all the other adult human beings such as a helpful assistant, an eager and practical aide, an occasional volunteer, a silent worker fixing the plumbing, the cook stirring and seasoning and bringing in food, the visiting nurse, and the passing postman. All these other adults who come in contact with the children are influential in some way and make a contribution. The children respond to them as helpful adults and are affected by *their* human values, their ways of speaking, their behavior, and their particular skills. All these adults, different from you, are important and contribute to children's learning.

A hefty plumber once came into the bathroom of a small nursery school one morning shortly after Christmas and promptly proceeded to operate the plunger. The busy three-year-olds stopped what they were doing and clustered around the workman who seemed so gigantic in stature and seemed to be doing such fascinating pushing and pulling and splashing with the plunger. The man worked in silent concentration; the children watched with a tense, muscular kind of pleasure. Finally Jimmy spoke for them all.

"Mister!" he called out, his face an expression of admiration and envy as he pointed to the plunger. "Did you get this for Christmas?"

The plumber chuckled kindly, touched by the children's genuine interest in his mundane job.*

The teacher, too, was impressed, but not merely by the cuteness of the child's spontaneous remark or his naive concept of the plunger as a glamorous object worthy of a Christmas gift. She was aware of the children's *attention* to the workman, their *study* of his tools of trade, and their *interest* in commonplace mechanics. The result of the plumber's visit was a respectful acquaintance with a workman, as well as observation of simple mechanics.

Other workers who serve the school — carpenter, milkman, window washer, garbage collector — can be similarly useful to the teacher and can help her understand children's responsiveness to other people, as we shall see in subsequent chapters.

One of the first concerns that parents and supervisors have about a preschool is the teacher's attitude toward children. We have heard and believe by now that a teacher must be personally interested in each child. But how do you show it? One way is learning the children's names as soon as possible and addressing each child by his name when speaking to him. This means not relying on the easy use of "honey" or "dear" which feels nice to use occasionally and not being satisfied with the impersonal group

*Jessie Stanton, formerly of Bank Street College, told this incident to me.

address "boys and girls." Using a child's name shows the teacher's attention to and respect for the individual and signifies personal interest. A routine task of taking attendance can be meaningful when you call a child's name and really look at him.

Knowing and using children's names means knowing them as individuals and leads to interaction with them. A teacher who is using her human assets in learning to know each child looks at his various strengths and weaknesses or vulnerabilities and discerns a call for help.

Sally is a little girl who speaks to you only with her eyes and to other children only haltingly. You may decide she is shy and perhaps slow or immature. But when you listen to her outburst with dolls and notice her activity in family play, you develop a different notion about her language ability, her social strength, and her feelings.

Andrew is a physically strong, friendly, and rambunctious boy who does not concentrate in quiet activities as other children seem to do. Also, he pays little attention when you try to direct him. You might decide that he is not getting ready for the "real school," and you may wonder how to elicit his response to more educational activities.

Then something noneducational, something in real life, happens. A large old ladder box in the play yard starts to creak and huge nails poke out. The first person to notice the box is the "inattentive" Andrew who reports the danger to you. While you are pondering who could fix it or where to get a hammer, Andrew tells the children (with emphatic shouts) not to get into the box, and he runs to get a hammer from a workman in another part of the school. He succeeds in this situation, making it clear to you that he is using his head as well as his skill. Apparently, this child is also capable of cooperative effort in hammering the nails and in turning the heavy piece of equipment for inspection on all sides, and he shows himself to be a leader.

Seeing for yourself how Andrew was able to recognize and respect a dangerous condition and act upon it, and how he concentrated and completed an important task, you gained considerable knowledge about this child. This actual incident in the play yard also caused the teacher to take stock of her program and her expectations of the other children. She decided that not only Andrew, but also others (the nice quiet ones) were responsive to physical, practical, and responsible activities.

Another important asset of the teacher as a human being, then, is an open eye and mind toward children and willingness to learn from them. To do this, you need to be a cultivated child watcher.

As a human being, you need not only to learn and grow in understanding, but also to feel successful in your job. You not only know that the children in your class are doing well, and that there are no complaints, but also recognize and enjoy the teaching activities. You appreciate the fact that when children look up to you for help you are able to give it. When they ask you many questions, you thoughtfully answer some and others you take as challenges. When children get quickly excited or tearfully upset, you have calming words and gestures that help protect and sooth. When you read a chosen story, sing a song with them, or share important news, they respond to you. They respond not with grown-ups' politeness and conventional words but with personal attention to you, with genuine emotion and imagination. Even if this happens once in a while, the effect from success is lasting; it makes you strive to continue eliciting genuine response.

What also helps you to feel successful is expressed recognition from your superiors in the job. Supervisory persons are often so concerned with solving problems or providing for regulations that they overlook the essentially constructive and successful activities of the teacher. They expect you to do well or they will tell you otherwise. While holding yourself accountable and taking stock of yourself as a teacher, it is human to seek from those in charge some practical appraisal and to want a little praise.

Sometimes you may have a bad day, but you need not feel devastated by it. An occasional setback is in the nature of human enterprise and is not destructive. With preschool children one bad day may throw light on the many good ones. You, the teacher, as a human being need to make certain that the good days outnumber the bad and to analyze the latter in terms of future pitfalls to avoid or overcome. This means you are learning from your own experience.

2 The Child Himself

From the point of view of the child, the most important "subject" is himself. The tangible parts and functions of his body are of intimate concern to him, though he may not know all the words for them. Any preschool child who comes to you is likely to know such words as *feet*, *hands*, and *nose*, but he is not likely to know such terms as *ankles*, *elbows*, and *nostrils*. Yet, since they pertain to him personally, he would enjoy knowing these words. By watching a child play and by listening and talking with him (without quizzing), a teacher can tell which words he knows and which ones she* should supply as needed so that he may learn them on the spot, without instruction.

The first warm days of the year children are likely to display their spring clothes.

"See my new shirt?" asks Mike. "It has short sleeves."

---

*I have used the pronoun *she* to refer to a preschool teacher because the phrase *he or she* sounds clumsy, and the word *he* would not be accurate since the female preschool teacher is obviously more common than the male. I trust, however, that (as treated in this book) the preschool teacher's human attributes, energy, and creativity transcend gender.

He inspects carefully the sleeves and the arms.

"The sleeves come only to this part," Mike continues as he knocks on one elbow with his fingers.

"Yes, the sleeves are above your elbows!" the teacher responds. "Same as Janet's."

"Elbows," Mike repeats, "these are my elbows!"

Elbows — what a discovery for a three-, a four-, or even a five-year-old. His enthusiasm is contagious to the whole class, and others check on the presence or visibility of their elbows. Soon the interest spreads to wrists and knuckles, to ankles and knees. At such a time songs and games that involve enumeration of body parts become more meaningful, popular, and creative. Also picture books with anatomical references can be especially interesting, such as Look at Me![1]

Naming, demonstrating, or having a pantomime guessing game about body functions can be very exciting and provide personal learning. You might even find it stimulating for children to invent rhymes when enumerating and demonstrating such functions; for example: thinking/winking, biting/fighting, napping/slapping, wiggling/giggling. Children enjoy rhymes and acting out words. Therefore, coordinating these two activities with learning how the body works is intriguing and rewarding to children.

"Why is it," asked a Russian five-year-old, "that when I drink milk and cocoa and tea — only tea comes out of me?"[2]

"This little bit of onion isn't going to make me cry!" boasted Allen, blinking as he peeled an onion and tried to control the tears.

Another youngster, startled by his own sudden sneeze, pushed the pepper mill away and then grinned knowingly.

Neither of these three children or the teacher can know the chemistry of urine color, the precise function of tear ducts, or the physiology of a sneeze reflex. But, recognizing children's observations and listening to their comments, the teacher can provide for more experiences, which in turn might correct misconceptions. Learning about power and control of their own bodies and their own selves is entirely appropriate for young children.

"I am a statue," announced Jill, becoming immobile for as long as she possibly could. What control and concentration it required!

[1]Marguerita Rudolph. Look at Me! New York: McGraw-Hill Book Co., 1967.

[2]Kornei Chukovsky. From Two to Five. Berkeley, Calif: University of California Press, 1963.

"This is how fast I can run!" called Johnny. Watch him! All the spunk and speed and strength of a little boy's body were in that run!

Equally strong is the cautious child, scheming to jump from a higher level than he has ever dared. He is scared, yet determined. Finally, getting closer and closer, he jumps and then spontaneously does it again and again. There goes a proud child!

From a child's point of view there are many curious and fascinating things to do with just one part of his body! With his breath he can blow away a paper, a feather, or a feathery seed; create a sphere from a limp balloon; cool hot soup; and warm chilled hands. He can make hand prints on wet sand or finger holes or scratches in the soil with his nails. He can use every appendage and his whole body to make shadows of different dimensions.

There is much *knowing* with the body and senses. Children enjoy enumerating important items that they know by sight, sound, smell, touch, taste, and also weight. Heaviness and lightness are attributes children know by picking up, holding, carrying, and balancing. What a challenge it is to pick up and carry or balance objects of different weights: a smooth, round armful of a pumpkin or a high stack of blocks; a rough bagful of sand or a half-pail of splashy water; a slippery book (or cardboard) on top of the head.

Thump! Ouch! Tom slid suddenly down a seesaw when his partner got off and another child much lighter than the one before mounted the opposite end. Tom was surprised, and only after repeated practice was he able to distinguish and judge weight differences with his body.

In the process of continued sensory experiences children learn how useful the senses are. Many tests that seem like play can be devised with children to help them become aware of the acuity of the senses, for example, a "Touch and Tell" game, which is not at all like "Show and Tell." For "Touch and Tell," a blindfolded child comes before the group and puts his hand in an attractively decorated bag containing small objects (stone, comb, spoon, pencil, etc.). He removes one of the items and tells how it feels to the touch (smooth, rough, pointy, etc.) as he uses sensory clues for guessing what the object is. This approach helps children search for and learn descriptive words and enjoy concentrating on finding out by touch. A similar game, "Don't Look But Listen," provides an opportunity for listening to a sound, without seeing the source, and determining the nature of the sound; for example: a ticking or an alarm-sounding clock, a stream of water poured into an empty or partially filled pitcher, paper or cloth being torn. How fascinating the isolated sounds seem and how pleased children feel to possess and to refine sound discrimination!

Practicing various personal powers, strengths, and skills offers much challenge to a young child's learning. He is ready to learn what the human voice is like by achieving different levels of whispers, shouts, calls, laughter, etc. He is excited by discovering the range of his own individual voice and the voice of the group as a whole.

The child is ready to learn about different muscle power involved in kicking a ball, lifting a chair, carrying a mop pail, using a pump, and using a fruit squeezer or even a bare hand for squeezing juice from a lemon. He is naturally aware of the muscle power of his limbs. The teacher can foster this awareness by noticing the foot power he uses in walking to school or the leg muscles he needs for running. She might praise his muscle strength in collapsing an empty milk carton that he whacks with his fist or steps on so that it will fit better in the trash can. A young child himself discovers how to control and direct his muscle power. When breaking sticks for "cargo" or for kindling, he learns to exert force to achieve a *snap*. When cracking a nut with a stone, he tries to control his force so as to crack the shell only. When a child gets satisfaction from using physical strength and receives teacher recognition for it, he feels acceptable as a whole person, pleased with himself, and happy to cooperate with the adult.

A five-year-old was playing in a city park after a storm. There were sticks and branches around. He started piling them in his wagon, breaking some to fit. The thin sticks snapped in his hands without much effort, but some branches were tough and he tried, without success, stepping on them. In response to a suggestion, he placed one of the thicker sticks on an incline and jumped on it. How thrilled he was with the success! He then experimented diligently with thicknesses of sticks, degrees of inclines, and differences in exerted force. This example of a child's discovery (with only a bit of help), using and learning from his own strength while playing, is typical of young children.

"I'll do it myself" is a most common expression (whether in words or in attitude) of children two to six years of age when they are free to say or to demonstrate what they mean. It has great meaning for growth and for learning. They want to do everything themselves and really be their own teachers. Children want to teach themselves and they can to a considerable extent.

The more things you can let a child do for himself, however inefficiently and even poorly on the first tries, the better he feels about himself as being worthy. In addition he becomes more encouraged to keep on trying and practicing with patience and persistence that seem amazing to adults. He succeeds more quickly in becoming skillful and in having enough competence to want to proceed to the next step. Yes, unless there is physical danger (a child has not had the experience to appreciate danger), you must let him do much for himself as soon as he wants.

Tasks a child can do include serving food, pouring a beverage, managing clothing, washing face and hands, trying to tie shoelaces, using scissors, using woodworking tools, and even washing and ironing some clothes under supervision. If he cannot do the complete job, he can still take part in self-help or self-service activities. Having a chance to do this makes him feel good because there is recognition of his interest. In one early childhood center a child chose a patch for torn pants and made a couple of stitches; another found a matching button to replace a missing one. A child feels great to have a hand or at least a finger in being able to take care of his own needs; it gives him an incentive to learn.

The teacher will find it useful to make a list of all things the three-, four-, five-, six-, or seven-year-olds can or are interested in doing alone for themselves. Then she sees that an adult gives them a chance or a little help and proper recognition.

Taking care of himself means also being responsible for waste he creates! Spills and splashes result not in punishment but in effective use of dustpan or sponge. Drippings and droppings, snips and cuttings are wiped and swept and go in the trash basket. With the teacher's consistent example young children can appreciate today's need for minimizing throwaways, reusing disposables, and diminishing waste. This is a personal and valid challenge and introduces young children to environmental protection.

Along with appreciating himself (the power of his brawn and brain), experiencing self-help, having a voice in managing his affairs, it is important for a child to have some possessions that are his very own with which he can be selfish. He needs his own things that belong just to him and that may even serve as an extension or representation of himself. Having his own box of crayons, recognizing and writing or trying to write his own name (in whatever size letters), having his own bag or box or hook or cubby in school give him assurance and security. It is absurd to expect children (and to admonish them about it) to share with others automatically or when told to do so *before* they have had possessions and a chance to enjoy them. Sharing for young children is difficult and is learned *slowly* from within.

Meg and her mother were very happy to come to nursery school, both beaming on entering the classroom in the morning and then looking around before parting and taking in every interesting nook and corner. It was still early in the year when Meg and her mother came to school with a special expression on their faces that meant "I have a surprise." Meg was clutching a big box.

"We were at the beach yesterday and collected these shells for the class," the mother hastened to inform the teacher. "It was Meg's idea!" she added with pride.

Indeed it was Meg's idea then, but now as the three of them touched and admired her beautiful new collection, she naturally refused to part with it. She clutched it close to her. Then, looking almost panicky, she whispered something in her mother's ear. The mother looked flushed and disappointed. Just a minute ago she felt pride in her child's virtue and now the same child, for no reason it seemed, was acting selfish and babyish.

"Oh, Meg, you mustn't take the box home!" the mother implored, not wanting to spoil the good impression she had made on the teacher in offering the collection. But Meg's feeling of wanting to keep the shells was strong, and she was rightfully adamant about it.

The teacher then thanked Meg for showing the shells and advised the mother to take Meg's own beautiful collection home. Subsequently the mother did see Meg's position of wanting to keep her new treasure. Later, Meg herself brought the collection to school "to stay for a while," which was a step toward still greater sharing.

When listening to the child, the teacher does not admonish him for being selfish. Instead she learns what the child enjoys and is capable of appreciating and how he gains self-respect, which will gradually enable him to respect others and eventually act in their behalf.

3 The Child's Family and Home

A young child leaving home for school is likely to bring some of the home with him — sometimes objects he is attached to, sometimes feelings about family, and sometimes maybe sorrows. How can a teacher tell?

One day Michelle arrived in nursery school sulking and turning an indifferent cheek to her classmates' friendly approaches. In response to the teacher's greeting, she crawled under the table and then tried to hide behind a chair, clearly removing herself from circulation in this lively, stimulating group in which she was usually an active member. She even stayed away from milk and cookies, which she usually enjoyed.

The teacher felt Michelle's sadness and confusion. She had already talked with the mother on the phone and was aware of the family trouble. This, the teacher felt, was cause enough for Michelle's strange behavior. Now the teacher had to remain a caring adult in charge of a group of children, responsive to the needs of all of them. She could not concentrate her sympathies upon one child and, therefore, she left Michelle alone. Being left alone in a friendly place, with friendly people, does not mean being neglected. So toward the end of the day Michelle recovered, responded to the teacher, and became her usual self.

What about Johnny whose troubles did not show in his behavior? The sensitive teacher saw the tenseness in Johnny's face and understood the message of unexpressed worry. She saw that other children's pleasures and movements were barely noticed by him.

Johnny's mother appeared early in the morning in a distressed state. She peeked anxiously at him through the window, surprised to find him "getting along all right," which is how she interpreted his subdued demeanor.

"He didn't want to go to school this morning . . . I had to practically force him," she sighed as she began to relate what had happened.

She said that Johnny had a warm relationship with his father and he was terribly upset when the father left on a business trip. She tried to console Johnny by saying "Daddy will be back in a few days." Johnny cried all the more, saying, "Daddy will never come back," and he would not listen. This had distressed the mother and she was indeed relieved by the impromptu conference.

A child of this age can be emotionally disturbed by family separation that is unacceptable to him. He is unable to understand the reasons and still less able to conceive of "a few days." If Daddy is not here now when Johnny wants him, then a few days is "never," an eternity. Grown-ups' words of persuasion carry no conviction.

Michelle's and Johnny's reactions to family disruptions demonstrate that a young child is very likely to come to school not only with a home problem, but also with some excitement, good news such as a family trip, or new mittens which a family friend knitted for him and which he does not want to remove. The teacher, with her humanness and sympathy, tries to discern the special meaning to the child of what he brings from home. Her very awareness and friendly presence can ease the distress or the excitement.

It is necessary for a teacher to have some knowledge of the child's family and his place in it. She may acquire it through the social worker, school director, or other staff member who knows the family. She may gain such knowledge during a friendly chat with the mother. Sometimes a purposeful get-together session with a small group of parents reveals important family concerns. An informal discussion may bring about parents' trust and enable them to be at ease with the teacher so that they do not hesitate to ask questions or to tell a teacher about important family happenings.

The modern teacher cannot have rigid notions of what constitutes a family. A family may not have two regular parents and yet be a close-knit unit. There may be instead a mothering, protective grandmother and a remote father. Or, as is happening more and more in our enlightened society, the parents may be adoptive parents instead of biological parents, and they may even be of a different race from the children. The teacher must recognize that, whatever the composition, this *is* the child's family where he gets his sustenance and security and toward whom he feels love and loyalty.

Little children can be loyal without reservation. Ralph was in a noisy cluster of children who were talking freely about their families.

"My father drives a truck," one child said.

"And my uncle has a taxi," reported another.

"Well, *my father*," Ralph proclaimed, "he's in jail."

The teacher made no judgment and neither did the children. What five-year-old Ralph knew about jails was that his father was there. Ralph was ready to be on his father's side wherever his father was.

While sitting on a park bench in a Russian city a few years ago, I observed a quiet elderly grandmother with a lively, bright three-year-old boy. Though neither said much, there was clear evidence of their secure relationship. Then a busybody old woman approached the boy and his grandmother.

"Do you love your grandma? Show me how much!" the garrulous woman, a stranger, said to the boy.

So the three-year-old hugged his grandmother.

"You must obey your grandma, do as she tells you," continued the woman in a more kindly tone. "Or else I'll take her away."

"But I am not going to let you take grandma," the little boy responded cheerfully.

"Well then," she said, "I'll take *you* to my house and keep you."

"I will not give *her* away, and I will not give away *myself!*" he said thoughtfully and decisively.

The Russian boy's loyalty to his grandmother is as meaningful as Ralph's loyalty to his father.

Children as well as the teachers in a preschool program benefit from contact with families. Visits of mothers, fathers, or other family members to the school are important occasions. A mother coming for a birthday celebration is impressive to the whole class.

"It's Marisa's birthday! We are going to have a *party*. And Marisa's *mother* is coming! *There* she is!" This was said with candid glances, turns of the head, and pointing fingers. Marisa's mother brought cupcakes and birthday napkins. The shy mother felt somewhat ill at ease, but the attention actually pleased her. There was a joyous excitement in the group of four-year-olds and clearly the visit of the mother was part of it.

Of course, when the school is run as a parent cooperative and each child's mother has her scheduled turn as a helping teacher, the presence of the mother is not a novelty. However, her contribution and influence as a caring adult are all the more important.

Mothers may join a preschool class on other occasions. They may be of special assistance with an excursion or a cooking or planting project. At the invitation of the teacher or the child, or because of her own desire, a mother may come just to observe. Her presence and her interest, while she is informally in the midst of the group, enhance the stature of her child, and contribute to the teacher's and the children's knowledge of the family.

A mother may bring a baby to the class if the brother or sister wants to *show* the baby to friends. Depending on the teacher's attitude, mother's and baby's presence could elicit the children's interest and provide a meaningful experience. One teacher invited a mother to nurse a baby in class. The teacher knew that the children had little or no familiarity with mothers nursing babies, but she believed this was a healthy, natural activity that would interest children. This particular mother had nursed her other children and was entirely comfortable nursing in the presence of others. What intense observation, puzzlement, and relevant remarks came from the children! The teacher felt that they were learning something new about mothers and babies and even understanding of the economic relationship of the two: the baby needs milk, he cries for it, the mother supplies it.

Other family members may also serve as educational resources. Mitchell's ten-year-old brother Michael, so big and tall by comparison with the still squatty preschoolers, came to demonstrate the care of a pet snake which he was lending to the school. The children were naturally fascinated by the snake, but they were spellbound by Michael and listened quietly to his explanation of the proper care and feeding of snakes. The teacher translated Michael's admonitions to the children, but Mitchell and the others were responding to Michael's feeling of protection more than to his words.

"It was nice to have a big brother visit us," the teacher said.

"I have an old grandpa!" boasted Tricia. "He could come."

The teacher will want to make a list of grandpas, grandmas, or visiting aunts who may wish to come to help, to do something special, or to play. The procedure of inviting family members is in itself a valuable communication for teacher and children.

After a teacher familiarizes herself with the family as a resource, she may invite a mother to cook something for the children (see Chapter 6) or to help with some simple sewing such as making needed pot holders, smocks converted from men's old shirts, or desired doll clothes or dress-up clothes. Another member of a family might be available to help with much appreciated construction or repair of a wagon, play house, or storage shed. Older siblings may have various scientific hobbies to share with the class.

In one school where the grounds were very limited, the class planted a vegetable garden in the backyard of one of the children, David, who lived just a block away. The class tended the garden from mid-April through June, leaving a rich harvest to be gathered later by David and his family. The family proved to be truly cooperative and later reaped the benefits themselves and made a special delivery of vegetables to David's classmates.

The teacher might also make use of artistic or musical family members. A mother (or other family member) might come in to read a book or tell a story. For the children this experience brings home life and school life closer together.

Another way of bringing home life to school life is by paying a visit to a child's home. Naturally, this can be done only when the particular child and his mother feel they want to invite a "gang of kids." Some mothers may need to be informed that for this kind of visit special house cleaning or elaborate preparation or "entertainment" is not required to make the event meaningful. If there are not enough chairs in the house, the floor is excellent for children to sit on for a snack, a game, or a song. If the child's home is a small apartment and a group of twenty or even fifteen is too big to squeeze in, two separate trips might be arranged, thus avoiding the mother's frenzy and the children's fatigue from overcrowding. The object of the home visit is to provide a truly social experience of hosting and guesting: the child host or hostess (together with mother) welcoming, maybe offering refreshments, saying hello and good-bye; and the guests receiving, enjoying, conveying pleasure in their own way rather than in a formal, uniform manner, and not overstaying the welcome. In such a project the teacher and the mother are sharing in planning, and both appreciate the meaning of the visit to the children.

Besides such direct experience in home-school relationships, young children need an opportunity to express feelings and ideas about family in imaginative play which usually takes place in the housekeeping area. This is a vital area in the classroom and deserves thoughtful and practical attention. First, what should this area contain? What kind of props and furnishings are needed to suggest or symbolize home and family? What materials can be managed independently and safely by children, can be orderly enough so that imaginative play can be satisfying, and can prevent housekeeping chaos? This area is private for the children, free from adult prying. Yet, the teacher needs to be able unobtrusively to hear or to look in for her own learning. The area should be partially walled or screened and contain basic household equipment, characteristic of the locale and thus familiar to the children. A table with chairs or benches that have a homey quality (different from the classroom furniture) where children may concentrate with various constructive materials. Utensils and props that are to be used for cooking, serving, eating, dressing, bedding, and baby care should be of good size which the children can handle securely. The small doll tea sets that are commonly seen in preschool classes are not adequate because they are easily dropped, scattered, and stepped on, which distracts from the flow of the dramatic play.

Equipment or furnishings should be placed in an orderly and logical (but not rigid) arrangement for the sake of efficient and independent cleanup. A simple, uncluttered arrangement helps children appreciate order. True, children themselves often enjoy mixing up things. They may deliberately put items in the wrong place: broom on table, frying pan in bed, and "baby" in the oven. During play, they may not seem to care about where things belong, from an adult point of view. The teacher should not require the children to be orderly and should not tell them how to play while they are imaginatively, creatively occupied. That would be an intrusion — even an invasion of privacy.

Yes, children do play in a complicated, imaginative, and messy way. To enable them to make a mess (which could be very meaningful), a place should be designated for this activity. The reality of cleanup when play is over does require efficiency and order. Giving children freedom in play does not negate the teacher's responsibility to offer children some standards: cleaning up dishes;

picking up clothes; arranging utensils in some order; placing an item of beauty in the home such as a tablecloth, a wall picture, or whatever item a child might choose or contribute.

In the housekeeping area there should be a place with good hooks or a chest or even a laundry basket for the dress-up clothes and a bed or two with pillows and covers (maybe a small patchwork quilt or colorful blanket). Whatever bedding is provided, it should not be just thrown in, piled haphazardly, and allowed to stay soiled. Dishes may consist of matching cups or mugs hung or stacked so that they are noticeable. Pots and pans should be visible in a definite place. A rug or a mat on the floor and maybe a rocking chair can add informal and inviting touches.

The teacher may have not only a certain reasonable arrangement ready when the children enter each day, but also some surprise for them in the house, such as this teacher often provided to indicate her support of dramatic family play. Hating to discard dead spring flowers in the room, the teacher shook all the lilac petals into a bowl and put it on the table in the housekeeping area. Children did take notice of this surprise, and after inspection and speculation of "what should we do with it?" they decided to "put the flower petals in the dolls' soup." Thus, "petal soup" became a family dinner dish!

Children's collections of nonpoisonous seed pods are used often to symbolize whatever food is meaningful to them. Therefore, a few jars or boxes and baskets of local natural materials should be available for children to select and incorporate into their imaginative play. Such play, through which children reflect their home life, provides an outlet for expressing family feelings and asserting themselves. During this play the teacher has an opportunity to learn more about a child, his home, and his family.

During a particular year or period, the home-school relationship may not be productive or positive as far as the teacher is concerned. She may meet with indifference rather than expected pride on the part of some parents. She may encounter resentment rather than cooperation with her projects. She may even find herself an object of criticism rather than of praise which she feels she deserves. Such criticism could be an occasion for a teacher's self-examination.

A preschool teacher needs the quality of patience, and sometimes of humility, to learn from parents. Having such qualities helps her know and enjoy the child and his family.

4 Animals In and Out of the Classroom

What is so important about animals* for little children in school? Ah, it is the *aliveness* of animals that matters to children.

When confronted with a stiff looking turtle, an unmoving, frightened frog, or a stationary beetle on a twig, children are likely to ask: "Is he real?" "Why doesn't he walk?" "Will he bite?"

Mere words of a teacher's reply do not constitute an answer. It takes direct and continued contact with living creatures for a child to make observations, to find some answers, to ask new questions, and to perceive aliveness.

Thrusting a lettuce leaf into the guinea pig's cage on the floor, Craig called excitedly, "He grabbed it from my *hand*! He's chewing it now."

Craig took a squatting position, watching the guinea pig intently. "He is looking at me!" he exclaimed.

Then he asked worriedly, "Why is he lying down?"

Eric watched a turtle contemplating a worm, then concluded, "I think the turtle is *thinking* about eating the worm. Will he eat it like 'pesgetti,' and roll it in?"

Eric demonstrated the act by using his tongue. Later, when the

*The local health department should be consulted about any prevalent animal diseases before bringing animals into the classroom.

turtle was completely in the shell, he wanted to know, "Where are his feet?" He waited to see the turtle's feet emerge.

"They are not feet," another child corrected. "They are paws (implying differentiation). And my dog has paws (thinking of similarities)."

Invariably, children notice and take an interest in eating habits of different animals, distinguish the shape of the droppings ("rabbits' are like raisins"), or observe the nature of locomotion ("the worm—he stretches"). But it is the feeding, especially if the creature eats out of the hand or drinks when given water, that brings such pleasure and fascination.

In the yard when the teacher said casually to the group of children, "the turtle doesn't have any water," three children at once picked up pails from the sandbox and dashed to the water fountain. Several others crowded around the play boat where the big box turtle resided. The three came, holding the splashing pails against their chests, and poured the water into a large garbage can lid that served as a water pan. As the tough turtle stuck its rough neck out and with impressive deliberation moved toward and into the water, the children of that group as well as turtle watchers from other groups clustered around the creature and held their breath in suspense. Although many of them had seen the turtle drink before, it still seemed a fresh or, at any rate, a different experience. Seeing the turtle bend its head at a special angle, immersing and holding it there, many of the children made corresponding head and neck motions. In a manner of speaking, they became turtles themselves.

An animal in the classroom, lobby, or yard is a major source of learning for all children. Each child gradually feels the other children's free involvement, becomes intrigued by the activities, and also notices the teacher's regard for the animal. Over a period of time, children respond in some way to the quality in the teacher's care of animals and the nature of her own interest.

Realistically, we cannot say that all teachers *usually* like animals or have practical experience and knowledge in the care of animals. Perhaps, the average teacher, irrespective of her education, does not appreciate significantly the strong appeal of animals to children or the educational meaning of animals in any preschool program. Also, some teachers, like other people, have little tolerance for most animals. Some even have aversions to animals. In their grown-up (and civilized) mind, insects are to be killed unquestionably, rodents are to be poisoned, farm creatures are to be identified in pictures, and wild animals (such as tigers roaring out of tanks) are known through automobile commercials. The teacher might have read a book or seen a film on the importance of studying animals, but knowledge gained this way alone seldom becomes part of one's attitude and behavior. As far as many teachers are concerned, animals in the classroom are not very welcome. Even less welcome than its presence is the animal's inevitable production of excrement.

As one teacher explained it, "I've put up with it when my children were in diapers, and that's enough."

"But look how much it means to the *children*," a colleague replied.

"Sure!" the teacher answered with a touch of scorn. "Plenty of other things mean much to the children. And there are important things I do as a teacher, without using my time for cleaning cruddy cages. But I am not telling you what to do. Keep animals by all means — just don't let them escape here."

Was she offering an educational argument or defending her own intolerance?

Yet, even if in some situations and for some teachers it is too difficult to have an animal in residence, children need not be denied some kind of contact. If a teacher is squeamish about a hamster or a mouse in the room, she may find herself quite accepting of a couple of small, quiet green turtles in a clean plastic pan and even learning to share the children's amusement with the agility of such small creatures. She may be petrified of a darting snake, even in a secure wire cage, yet feel comfortable watching darting goldfish in a tank and noticing the children's pleasure at sprinkling food upon the water and their imitations of the fishes' mouthy motions.

From another classroom in her school the teacher might borrow an animal for an hour now and then, or her group (a few at a time) may visit. If there is a tree near the building, a bird feeder could be placed outside the window. What a privilege for children to watch a feeding bird to see at close range its power, its precision, its persistence! Even if there is only a dirty park nearby, children may spot a pigeon there. No doubt a flock of pigeons may rush and peck at any handout.

A teacher may obtain (from the woods in autumn or from a special store) a dry cocoon. In the spring a moth is born, emerging miraculously from the small, dark inside and requiring *no feeding* from any one! Few other sights elicit as much awe and wonder from children and adults as the color and pattern and flutter of a moth!

Because animals vary so widely in kind, size, and habitat, there will surely be some type of animal neighbor wherever a preschool is located: a land of permafrost, a desert, the shore of a pounding sea, an asphalt city slum, or a spacious field of green. An interesting notion to explore here is the *variety, prevalence, adaptability, survival,* and *ecological* relation of animals everywhere in the world. It is safe to say that even if there are laws against keeping animals in schools, if some adult is petrified of certain kinds of animals, if the classroom is small, or if there is no spot in the curriculum emphasizing animals, a teacher can still make (however superficial) an assessment of the environment and discover what living things are around. She can find out what they do and how helpful or in some situations how harmful they may be. An earthworm burrowing in the ground or a ladybug eating aphids on a rose bush is helpful, while a worm hidden in wrapped green leaves is harmful.

In a poor section of a southern town, children on their way to a Head Start center captured some grasshoppers on the dirt road. "Hopper grasses" they called them. After words of pride in their own prowess and success in capturing, they admired the insects jumping and concentrated on observing the big legs and other features. They took the creatures into their play and made houses for the grasshoppers with their building blocks. The children kept the creatures in creative captivity throughout the day, using more space and equipment outdoors, making comments within the teacher's hearing, and asking questions. Inevitably the grasshoppers escaped, causing excitement and dramatic disappointment for some, as well as providing a lively topic of conversation for children and adults. This natural encounter with an ordinary insect in their own neighborhood led to interest in other creatures, as was shown in the children's questions about the grasshoppers' food and grasshoppers' being food themselves. The teachers, rather than conveying their special knowledge or instructing the children, were accepting of the children's interest and shared in their learning.

Here is another spontaneous encounter, this time in a well-to-do suburban nursery school. In September children picked up fallen apples in the yard. The teacher helped with the washing and the cutting, in preparation for eating.

Suddenly the children saw a pink wiggle on the white, seemingly solid inside!

"How did he get in?"

"Where is his home?"

"Does he have a mother?"

Nobody really understood the teacher's tentative answers, but everyone had the answer to "What does he eat?" The children enjoyed eating the good parts of the apples and, just as much, the discovery of the live creatures inside. The group collected the worms in paper cups, counted them, let them loose, and watched them. They distinguished the dark heads of the worms and gave them chunks of apple to eat. Some children inspected "spoiled parts" of the apples, speculating on the worms' work. They all remembered the experience later and looked for worms inside other edibles, clearly impressed with the animals' adaptability rather than the harm to people's food. The wisdom of the teacher was not to ignore the children's curiosity or discourage them by such remarks as "Don't touch the worms!" or "Throw the apples away!"

In one cooperative kindergarten the teacher was unable to keep any animals because of building regulations. So she made elaborate arrangements to transport the class to an agricultural college in the neighboring town for a "special trip." However, this teacher, along with her colleagues and parents, did not recognize the benefit of a farm next door. "They are not nice people there," she told the children. True, there was an impenetrable high fence surrounding the farm, and the owner had a reputation for being crude and unfriendly. However, there were also unique sounds emanating from the neighboring enclosure: frequent bleating, occasional braying, and commonly heard clucking and loud crowing. There was also evidence of interesting business, customers arriving to purchase eggs. When the teacher realized this, she found reason to make contact. A small delegation of children with an adult went to purchase fresh eggs and take a look at the farm. Because they had come on business, they were readily admitted. After that the farm visit became a most popular weekly school errand. In addition to eggs the children brought back clumps of sheep wool, bunches of chicken feathers, and a strand of . . . "Is it really horse hair?"

In one school the teacher learned that a mounted police station was in a neighborhood park. The class made several visits to the station and shared some carrots with the civilized, dignified, controlled animals, admired their stature, and learned from the policemen about the horses' work and how the horses were cared for. Children returned to school with small quantities of oats that had been scooped out of a big barrel. Children and the teacher came away with a real feeling about the horses and also learned the meaning of the expression "horsepower." What a big lesson for four- and five-year-olds from big animals. But small animals, too, have power and significance in their being.

In one nursery school there was a virtual invasion of ants one spring. Of course, the ants had to be wiped off from all the surfaces, emptied out of all containers, swept from cracks and corners and out of doors. The teacher and children engaged in vigorous housecleaning. However unwelcome as the ants were as residents in the room ("We don't want the ants to eat our food," a child said.), their liveliness and their sheer numbers did not escape the children's notice and did stimulate thoughtful comments. So the teacher kept a few ants in soil in a glass container, and the children watched, fed, and befriended the tiny creatures. They regarded the insects' work and movement; they used a magnifying glass to better see the body parts, and with the teacher looked up "Ants" in several books, even in an encyclopedia. They looked at pictures of ants, enthusiastically recognizing them as a result of their own experience. A special sense of appreciating the value of ants as good food for many animals (big bears and small moles) was gained by the teacher and children alike.

Apparently aware of the teacher's interest in small animals, Eric one morning handed her a paper bag with—the reader would never guess what.

"I found it in my bathroom, and my mother hollered," Eric said.

It was a shiny-skinned cockroach. Indeed a most interesting, mobile creature to look in on and to study in a jar (if an adult's revulsion did not intrude)! The teacher, of course, felt compelled to explain to Eric's mother that, by bringing the cockroach to school, her son was following a scientific impulse.

Keeping animals temporarily has its advantages, and a teacher can be more tolerant when she knows that the visit will soon be over. Sometimes arrangements can be made with pet shops or farms to buy baby chicks or ducks at Easter time and to return them in two or three weeks. By that time they will have grown and changed noticeably and provided the whole class with much entertaining learning, with fun in naming them, with need to change routines to give regular care to the creatures. By that time, too, the teacher will have assumed and recognized responsibility not only for the animals, but also for the children's education from the experience.

Keeping animals confined and controlled for the benefit of humans may have philosophical drawbacks. Some people cannot appreciate or even accept any birds in a cage; the unnaturalness of captivity seems to border on evil. Some teachers think it is wrong to make an animal helpless and keep it in a locked cage like a prisoner! However they are sympathetic to animal encounters outdoors and to visiting animals living on farms, in ponds, at zoos, and at other locations.

The Navajos in Arizona are devoted to domestic pets (sheep, ponies, dogs, cats), but consider it a sacrilege to remove any animal from the place where it lives—whether it be a lizard, a toad, or some strange bright beetle. Why? They explain slowly and thoughtfully that an animal you do not know may hurt you or make you ill with unknown poison, and you may hurt the animal that did you no harm. You must watch and study and care about creatures where they really live, where each one is at home. "You will then find much to learn," say the Navajo Indians. What can we say in reply?

Other people's objections to caging animals may be a result of important personal experience. In one public school first grade in a poor section of the city, the teacher was successful in keeping a healthy, pregnant white rat in a comfortable cage in class. The teacher was pleased with the children's enthusiastic response, especially when the abundant litter arrived. But the distressed, irate parents who had suffered from rats in their homes did not share the children's enthusiasm or accept the explanation that the children were writing their own primer about the rats. To the parents the rats were not an academic matter at all! They wanted no association with rats on any terms!

It is understandable why a teacher or a director preparing a curriculum for a preschool program needs to engage in some philosophical reflection about kinds of animals and ways of including them in their plans. Most children in any preschool group are ready and willing to keep some animals as part of school.

Animals which are willingly (not grudgingly) cared for seem to give the classroom a certain happy tone. There may be lively sounds of squeaks and scratches in the room. There may be children's activity in behalf of animals, or expression of curiosity, or protective concern or amusement at animal's behavior, all of which add to the interest and liveliness of children and of the room in general. Some child or teacher bringing animal food from home contributes to an atmosphere in which there is caring, helping, and sharing. Children absorb such things. Of course the responsibility, the work, and the understanding of keeping an animal are all clearly the teacher's. However, she is at all times aware of sharing her activities or chores, as well as her understandings and feelings, with the children. She must accept the children's partnership, not just assign duties to them.

Making a *home* for any animal requires constant attention and study. Some animals, such as guinea pigs and box turtles, can be kept in large, deep, open boxes for children to see directly, touch, or take out once in a while for an individual child to hold and pet. The more agile climbers, such as hamsters or gerbils, need to be in a see-through, securely latched, and covered cage containing devices for exercise. Children can observe the animal's food preferences, his ways of moving, resting, and using space, and his need for a hiding spot. They can take part in putting fresh papers and cedar shavings in the cage for a gerbil or soil and rocks in the box for the turtle, as well as in removing the waste and replenishing food and water. With the teacher's guidance, the animal's home is checked periodically to see if it is satisfactory in size, cleanliness, and provisions for feeding, resting, hiding, and playing. When everything is found to be "all right" with the animal, the teacher feels all right, too. Without being formally taught, the children become familiar with animal physiology and practical work pertaining to eating, drinking, elimination, activity, and rest.

But what happens when everything is *not* all right? What then?

A small turtle disappeared. The result: the children engaged in frantic search everywhere, but in vain. Then the turtle reappeared. The result: great rejoicing, followed by sober, critical appraisal of the animal's home.

A child left the cage door open and Little Gray School Mouse escaped, swishing across the large classroom, causing instant alarm, and causing cries and shrieks of "Catch him! Catch him!" Such activity induced the teacher to crawl on the floor and capture the creature (something she had never done before). Seeing the teacher breathless and disheveled, and not entirely pleased with the episode, each child protested, "I didn't open the door!" "I didn't do it either!"

The children discovered one of the class pets, a half-grown duck, "sitting down" in the yard, apparently unable to walk because of an injured foot. Not only did all the group cluster sympathetically and inquisitively about the injured duck, but also a companion duck remained motionless, standing by. With deep appreciation the children and teacher realized that the other duck *would not* walk as long as "his friend" could not. Contacting the veterinarian, taking the duck to the hospital, and bringing it back with a splint on its leg took priority over *all* other school matters.

"But what if something worse should happen?" the reader might now ask. "What will *children* say when an animal . . . well —dies?" Yes, grown-ups usually worry and are at a loss about what to do or say that would be right in the eyes of children and that would cause them the least distress or preferably no distress. This seems unrealistic, for death is an inevitable encounter for the living, and young children take it on their own level, *differently* from grown-ups. It is indeed difficult for any one to explain death. In order to be sensitive to children's feelings and try to be practical toward the task at hand, it is important for the teacher to listen to children, observe them, and have some understanding of what a dead animal may mean to them.

A young nursery school teacher came into the director's office with a confused, unnatural expression on her face.

"There is a—hum—dead gerbil in our room," she said to the director. "Shall I ask the custodian to take him away? Or do you want to do something about it?"

This teacher had warm feelings for each child in her class and intelligent interest in every aspect of learning that went on in the group. However, she could not bring herself to handle animals, dead or alive; she only tolerated their presence for the children's sake.

"Frankly," the teacher added anxiously, "the sooner it's out of the room . . . the children don't seem to be a bit interested anyway. Nobody came up to the cage or said anything."

She spoke quite rationally. Still, the director was not convinced of the children's indifference. She went into the room and took the cage from its corner and placed it near the children.

"I want to see your gerbil," she said to whoever was within hearing distance.

Immediately, a couple of children also wanted "to see." When they asked what was the matter with the gerbil, the answer was: "What do you think?" A number of thoughtful answers were given by the group who by now had gathered around the gerbil: "He is sleeping." "He is resting." "He is sick." "He can't move." "Maybe he is dead."

Leslie nodded, confirming the last answer, "He is dead all right."

"Let's see him," some children said.

When the dead gerbil was placed on the table, a little boy moved him gently with a finger and said seriously, "See — he can move. He's not dead."

Many children wanted to touch the dead gerbil and they offered proof of death. Some assumed the gerbil would be cured with food and water. Others wanted burial like the "Dead Bird" in the story by Margaret Wise Brown.[1] Some were skeptical about finality.

"Let's see what happens by the time we have snack. Let's wait till then," insisted Leslie.

It was evident by now, especially with Leslie's refrain, "He's dead all right," that attention to the dead animal had lasted long enough.

"You are right," the adult in charge said to the children with finality. "The gerbil is dead. And we can bury him in a good spot in our yard when we go out." And they did!

There was so much said by the children as expressions of thinking, questioning, judging, feeling, and practicality about burying. The teacher who was present all the time was very moved by the children's full response and appreciated the educational value of the experience, although she herself could not have managed that kind of emotional and intellectual involvement *and* the handling of the animal.

When encountering death, children become quickly concerned with causes. Hearing one child express an opinion, others are stimulated to put forth theirs.

"I wonder what happened?" the teacher asked when she and the children saw that one of the two hamsters was unmistakably dead.

[1] Margaret Wise Brown. *Dead Bird.* New York: William R. Scott, Inc., 1958.

"The other hamster tried to bite him," a child said.

"Maybe that other hamster scratched him," responded another.

"Maybe that's the father and he punched . . ." The children were enumerating ways of doing harm, ways that were presumably familiar to them.

"He's bleeding—that's why he is dead," was a remark from several others, noting blood as being both evidence and cause of death.

As in the case of the gerbil, some children also suggested cures: "Take him to a doctor." "Take him to a hospital."

Some children respond quickly and openly, wanting to know what a dead thing is. Others are hesitant and silent; then later they feel moved to have their say. Some children feel sad or distressed, and the teacher needs to be sympathetic without giving the child undue attention or identifying with the child, recognizing that distress is not a permanent state.

An encounter with animal death may well be distressing or even tragic. But can or should children be sheltered from all distress? Is not facing up and living through some stresses and distresses part of growing up? Would not animal death when the knowledge is shared with friends be a preparation for possible later experience with human death?

If animals of both sexes are kept for a length of time, children might observe them doing what comes naturally—mating. In which case they may ask questions, make comments, or say nothing after either watching the act or giving it a passing look.

In one class there were two big "clunky" box turtles.

"Look," Richard called to the teacher, "one turtle is on top of the other!"

The teacher came to look and so did several children. Sure enough, the two turtles were in one mound like a pile of rocks. There was no visible activity and the children's comments had to do with relative bigness, weight, and position of the turtles. It was obvious to the teacher that the children had no notion whatsoever that the turtles were in a mating position. But she was interested in whether any of the children had an interpretation of this animal behavior.

"Why do you think the turtles are staying like this?" she asked.

Now the children watched more closely and thoughtfully.

Finally Richard said slowly: "I think they are being friendly."

The teacher merely nodded. "Nothing wrong with that answer," she thought and she did not spoil it with her reaction. Without further intrusion, she and the children left the turtles alone. That was enough "lesson." Further verbalizing, pointing, or prying was unnecessary.

When there is active mating taking place, children may notice and show more interest, and the teacher may be asked questions. Like any adult she may not be sure that preschoolers *ought* to know what mating is, or if they do, she would rather that somebody else (a specialist on the subject) explain it. Adults are likely to read human sexuality into children's questions and assume that children will want to know more and more, and that there will be no stopping them. But actually mating is not *that* important to children. An adult needs to listen to the meaning in a child's question.

"Why are the squirrels chasing each other?" asked one boy.

"They like to do it (meaning chasing is a desirable activity)," said a little girl.

Five-year-olds watching rabbits at close range in an unfamiliar activity asked the teacher, "What are they doing?"

The teacher looked at the children and answered directly: "That's called *mating*."

Then she realized that the strange word did not mean anything to the children and that it really did not constitute an answer.

While she reflected, another child asked: "What's *mating*?"

"It's a way of getting two bodies close together," the teacher responded, trying to be specific and accurate insofar as the act observed by the children was concerned.

This kind of questioning and answering would apply to similar activities of other animals: guinea pigs, chickens, even flies. It is the purpose and the pertinence of the children's questions that should give purpose and direction to the answer. If a pregnant animal is observed, children can begin to become aware of the biological female and the sequence of mating, pregnancy, and birth. Preschool children, ages three to six, are not able to listen to explanations on conception or fine sexual distinctions. Those are abstract matters which they cannot understand.

On a television program intended to show sex education in the preschool years, a teacher read the picture book *All About Eggs*[2] to a live audience of preschoolers. When there was a mention

---

[2] Millicent Selsam. *All About Eggs*. New York: William R. Scott, Inc., 1952.

of *dogs* having eggs (from which another dog will come), one child interrupted in a voice of experience: "They don't have eggs. They don't lay eggs. Dogs have *bones.*"

The preschooler's inability to grasp the biology of sex roles is clearly illustrated in Chukovksy's *From Two to Five:* "In reply to information that he came out of his mother, a four-year-old boy commented, according to *his* logic: "I knew it! If daddy had given birth to me, I'd have a mustache."* For children of this age the immediate, the tangible is what matters.

When the school pet rabbit who was "big and fat — she had babies inside" gave birth, the older nursery school children immediately noticed the emergence of the litter and at once proceeded to count and recount the seven bunnies. This was difficult as the mother kept concealing them. The teachers were right there, making sure the children learned the first important lesson, not to interfere and keep hands off. How quickly they understood and remembered the mother's belligerence and her total care and protection of the newborn. The children noticed not only the smallness, helplessness, and cuteness of the baby bunnies, but also their development in only a couple of weeks. Also, they noticed that "the mother is not so mean any more." She hid the babies less and let them run around more and more. Thanks to rabbit precocity, the babies soon matured, were interestingly active, and could be held and petted with no objections from the mother!

The rabbit family provoked considerable class discussions about necessary protection of babies and about controls and timely freedom for children! They concluded that the rabbit was a good mother. The teachers concluded at the end of the school year, when homes had been found for the grown rabbits, that all the extra work for them had been worthwhile. Nothing else could have provided greater pleasure and deeper learning for all: birth, parenthood, growth and development; mathematical exercises ("two are gone, so there are five bunnies left"); much practical work, including harvesting of plantain and dandelions; regard for school as a place so exciting you could hardly endure vacation; and much more. Every teacher will, of course, make her own conclusions as to what the grown-ups and children in the school learn together as a result of having animals in their midst.

*From *From Two to Five* by Kornei Chukovsky. Berkeley, Calif.: University of California Press, 1963.

5 Breaking Bread: Customs and Pleasures of Eating

You, a teacher of little children, in whatever kind of a school or group, have by now made some self-examination of your own interests and values as a human being. You have focused your attention on the young child himself and his needs, powers, and individual propensities. You have regarded sympathetically the child's family and home, relating them to his life in the classroom. You have considered bringing animals to your premises, thereby enlarging your own awareness and learning and bringing larger aspects of living into the child's everyday life. All those are areas common to early childhood experiences and learning with which the teacher has to concern herself. Another area of common experience for all children is food and eating. Food and eating are essential for the nutrition of growing children, but frequently their potential for rich and lasting learning is overlooked.

Almost any food has an immediate sensory appeal: seeing, smelling, tasting, biting, and definitely handling; all are basic to early childhood ways of learning. Different kinds of foods are easily brought in by adults or children. Unusual or unfamiliar food is to become acquainted with: perhaps a puckery persimmon that changes in time to edible softness, a pomegranate with countless brilliant seeds, or an unsliced long crusty loaf of French bread — so different from the standard American sliced, soft kind. Familiar food is to notice more and know better: a hand of green bananas turning yellow in the sunlight and then such fun to peel; pale green tomatoes turning all red in the same sunlight, and then so good to eat; or a big apple, dry and shiny and red on the outside, surprisingly juicy and white on the inside with hidden, dark, slippery seeds to be counted. Of course, there is food for regular eating time: snacks that are satisfying and interesting to handle and eat; appetizing breakfasts that are appropriate for a particular community; or a varied nutritious main meal with company of children and company of congenial sharing adults.

If eating in your program consists of pleasantly served, nutritious food with relaxed conversation between children and adults in a cheerful atmosphere, consider it an important achievement! Not many programs have it.

What does actually happen when an unfamiliar food is brought in for the group? What kind of learning takes place?

One of the children had received a coconut from a vacationing relative. When he brought it to school, no one was sure what it was since it was encased in a tough fiber coating which the children had never seen. Finding out how hard and tough the covering was and trying to break it occupied the children for two days. They used all the tools at their disposal: saw, hammer, screwdriver, and rocks. Cutting and striking and whacking brought no results, though there was tremendous satisfaction in the aggressive activity. Failure did not discourage the children; instead, it whetted their determination to break the coconut open. When a discussion took place about possible ways of opening the coconut, the teacher guided them to a solution.

"How do you think monkeys in a coconut tree open a coconut?" she asked, watching the challenge and amusement on the children's faces.

Someone suggested and someone rejected biting and hitting, but the idea of throwing it met with approval from many children. The teacher then assigned three of them to take turns hurling the coconut onto a paved area. Soon they succeeded in making a crack in the shell. How fascinating the occurrence of the crack was to all the children. How thrilling the operations of measuring and straining the liquid, though only a few ventured to taste it, and what undivided attention to the teacher's division and the cutting of the coconut meat, which all the group enjoyed as a special treat.

Those children had an unusual opportunity to engage in hard work in order to obtain the food they wanted. They were also propelled by the curiosity to see what was *inside* this strange, rough object. Could it really be food? The children especially liked using different tools and their own muscle power. They also noticed the different elements in one kind of food: a protective tough coating; the dry, hard brown shell; the crunchy, sweet white part that you eat; and the surprising liquid. The teachers were clearly aware of the children's involvement and learning from a strange food that elicited response and brought about rewarding activity.

Children and teachers can become also involved in activity and learning with some quite ordinary food.

After everyone in the group had enjoyed coloring eggs at pre-Easter time, there were a few cooked and raw white eggs left over, those spare ones which the teacher had brought just in case.

"Hard-boiled eggs are nice for a snack," the teacher thought. "Children could cut them in quarters and arrange on a plate to pass around . . ."

Giving the egg snack more thought, however, the teacher realized that many of those curious, active four-year-olds could have an interesting time investigating the exterior and interior of eggs. She remembered the brown eggs at home and decided to bring them to school to add to the others in order to stimulate observation and investigation.

Bringing anything to class, presumably for the children, always attracts attention, and the basket of white and brown eggs on a table with nothing else was no exception. The group soon clustered around the table, peeking and poking into the basket and asking innumerable questions: "Were the eggs brought for coloring? Why were they there? Could the eggs be eaten? Where did the brown ones come from? Were *they* good to eat?" The teacher realized these children were not familiar with brown chicken eggs.

"Do you think the white eggs and brown eggs are the same *inside*?" she asked.

The choral answer was "No" followed by an urgent, "Let's see! Let's see! Let's break them open!"

Just then a mother and child came into the room, and they were promptly drawn into the suspenseful scene with the eggs in the basket.

"Are these eggs raw or cooked?" the mother asked.

"Could you tell without breaking them, Mrs. Mateo?" the teacher asked her.

"I ought to," Mrs. Mateo answered.

She picked up several of the eggs one at a time, turning each from side to side, as she mentally judged the weight, rubbed the surface, and tried to differentiate the texture of the shell.

"This one must be raw," she said tentatively. "It seems lighter . . ."

"Break it open; then you'll see," a child advised helpfully.

"I know—I just remembered what my mother used to do!" Mrs. Mateo suddenly exclaimed. "You spin the eggs to tell if they are cooked."

The children had never seen such a performance and the teacher had only a vague notion about it. Mrs. Mateo spun the eggs on the smooth table, studying the difference in velocity. The teacher and the children also took turns spinning an egg and noticing differences.

At last Mrs. Mateo concluded: "See how fast this one spins! That's the hard-boiled."

She put this white egg aside.

"And this one hardly moves," she said, giving a twist to one of the brown eggs.

The children were now indeed eager to see each of the two eggs broken open into a separate clean colored bowl. Mrs. Mateo was discernibly nervous and then relieved that the fast spinning egg was cooked and the other raw as she had predicted.

The children however concluded something else! To them the different colored eggs were different on the inside as *they* had thought. At this point the teacher produced a raw white egg, breaking it open in still another bowl in order to correct the children's misconception. They could now see that no matter what color the egg was on the outside, it was the same on the inside.

"Put them together!" a little girl suggested, and the teacher poured one of the raw eggs into the bowl with the other egg. "You can't tell which is which."

The teacher removed the raw eggs, placed them in a bowl, and took them to the kitchen in order to attend to the cooked ones in preparation for a snack. She said good-bye to Mrs. Mateo and thanked her for helping out with the study of eggs.

"Well—I can see there is a lot I don't know about eggs," Mrs.

Mateo replied as she left with an unanswered question: "Why *doesn't* a raw egg spin?"

Before shelling the eggs the children practiced some more spinning and noticed that "eggs are not round. Eggs have points." They noticed, too, that the yolk of a hard-boiled egg was round and speculated on the reason, the forces determining its shape.

What a *happening* the leftover eggs proved to be! What unexpectedly rich learning! It came apparently from flexible planning and spontaneous involvement and inquiry. As the teacher was reflecting on the children's responses, she was uncertain whether they still held to their misconception about brown eggs. So she brought cooked brown eggs to school another day.

"These are the same," some children stated. "Will they be raw inside?"

But other children remembered the spinning test as an indicator. After the eggs were broken open, the children were satisfied that hard-boiled brown eggs were the same as hard-boiled white eggs. Some thought the taste was the same; others said brown eggs tasted better.

Other familiar foods can be important subjects of sensory experiences on a young child's level of scientific investigation, provided it is conducted in an informal setting which can be called a laboratory. What constitutes *familiar* differs, of course, with locality or community, as well as with ethnic preferences. Lima beans in pods for instance were everyday food for children in a Georgia town. They were quite adept at opening the rough pods with fingers and fingernails. Their chief interests in preparing the butter beans for a meal was in the cooperative organized labor — in counting the beans in each pod after guessing the number, in measuring the volume of pods and of shelled beans, and naturally in eating them. But children of similar age in a suburb of New York City did not know what lima beans were and also were unable to tear the pods open, finally resorting to using scissors. Many of these children were hesitant about eating the beans. A teacher who does not live in the same community as the children must keep in mind that what is familiar to her may not be at all familiar to the children in her class.

One teacher, after hearing a number of the children mention having orange juice for breakfast, decided to have orange juice instead of milk in school for the midmorning snack. Just as she had expected, the modern three- and four-year-olds, brought up on canned and frozen foods, did not know that orange juice can be squeezed out of a whole solid orange, although they had eaten cut juicy parts of oranges. In reply to the teacher's question "Where do we get orange juice?" the logical answers were: "From a can." "From the 'frig'." "From a bottle." Being able then to obtain a small quantity of tasty juice from a large heap of oranges was a very interesting technical operation. While using a hand squeezer, the children discovered a working muscle in the hand and the application of that muscle power, and they realized that through their own work they produced something for themselves. When they begged to do it again, the teacher could see that the process was as important as the product and that a common food was a natural subject for sensory learning.

Another teacher also had something similar in mind when she arranged a tasting lesson for her kindergarten class of twenty-three children after reading about sensory learning in an official curriculum guide, which she wanted to follow dutifully. First she made an announcement: "Today we are having a tasting lesson." Then she introduced Mrs. Smith, one of the mothers who had come to "assist us," and asked two monitors to distribute paper cups and plastic spoons to the sitting, receptive children. At the same time Mrs. Smith removed from a paper bag two familiar cartons of cottage cheese, the sight of which did not elicit any expression of pleasure from the children. The teacher held up the cartons for the class to view and asked them to raise their hands if they knew what was in the containers. Many hands shot up vigorously, but as always only one was lucky to attract the teacher's attention. All other hands limped down while the lucky child gave the correct answer. The teacher then proceeded with the lesson by *telling* the children that cottage cheese was a food, that it was "good for you," and that it contained alphabetical vitamins.

"Who can tell me what cottage cheese is made from?" the teacher then queried.

Again many hands shot up vigorously and another child was chosen to give a correct memorized answer: "From milk," which made the teacher feel proud.

"Did you hear that?" exclaimed the teacher, turning to Mrs. Smith. "Isn't Linda a smart girl?"

Then, changing her condescending expression, the teacher instructed the helping mother to serve a couple of spoonfuls to each child while she herself told the children to "eat it all up." The mother went about her task dutifully and silently as though administering a prescribed medication. A number of the children were clearly reluctant to eat the cottage cheese. Some ventured to say that they had already tasted it at home and did not like it. A few surreptitiously disposed of it under the table or in their napkins. Some children ate all their portions just to end the tasting lesson.

This teacher did not regard children's *pleasure* (or her own) as important in knowing food, nor did she seem to regard children's initiative and activity as prerequisites for learning. The only time they had used their hands was to raise a hand to answer a question.

What might this teacher have done instead to give the children experience in tasting inexpensive nutritious cottage cheese? Let us speculate!

She might have involved the children in some of the work and given them responsibility. Two or three children (with the mother's supervision and company) could have put the cheese in a bowl brought from home and used an attractive spoon for stirring. Those same children could have actually determined the taste and indicated improvement: "Needs a little salt," or "It should be sweeter." Sprinkling sugar into the cottage cheese would have immediately meant improvement to any child. Then, since cottage cheese is colorless and limp, a jar with bright jelly and a dish with dark, chewy raisins could also have been provided. Each child could have walked up to the serving table with his paper cup and *served himself* a desired portion of cheese with perhaps a teaspoon of jelly or a few raisins on top. One plain cracker could also have been added easily enough and would have made the tasting lesson more inviting. The result would have been enjoyable eating and a treat, not a nutritious treatment by the teacher. From such an experience the children would have likely gained appreciation of cottage cheese without the stress and strain and inhibition of a formal lesson.

Depending on the extent of school-home contacts, it could be quite natural to invite a family member to contribute his or her expertise or just good experience with food, and thus help the teacher extend children's knowledge and provide an interesting eating activity. For this, the teacher needs some acquaintance with prevalent popular foods, with available skillful family members, with stores stocking appropriate supplies.

A non-Indian teacher in a kindergarten near a reservation learned about a local staple food "fry bread" and found out how good it was when freshly made. Wanting to really partake of a local food at its best, she arranged for an Indian mother to come to the kindergarten to make the "fry bread" for the children's lunch. With the help of the assistant teacher who was also a local Indian, the mother handled the ingredients and utensils in an authentic way which she had learned from family tradition. Seeing all the stirring, hearing the sizzling, and sniffing the familiar appetizing smell, the children got ready for lunch in happy anticipation. The teacher thus shared in their satisfaction with a traditional food as she ate the "fry bread," exchanging pleasantries and thanking the mother for her important contribution.

In a different community, a grandmother of one of the children came to the class to make her specialty, potato pancakes. Her grandson informed the other children that they are "the best pancakes in the world." Eating on that day meant not only acquaintance with potato pancakes (not all the children were familiar with this dish) but also acquaintance with Danny's grandmother and pleasure in a different seating arrangement in a "partyish" atmosphere with everyone at one big table. Some children, finding the words euphonious, chanted: "Please / pass / potato / pancakes!" It was evident from their practical comments that the ingredients of the pancakes and the grandmother's work in their behalf did not escape their notice. However, the experience turned out to be valuable for its good sociability, which often goes along with eating, and it also stimulated creative language.

Any teacher-guided project or activity with food has unexpected side benefits that include a particular kind of learning and pleasure.

An American teacher with Chinese upbringing promised the children to cook her favorite Chinese rice dish for them. She kept her promise and brought to school special ingredients and utensils. With the help of an assistant as well as of some children, she prepared the dish in an authentic Chinese way for a late morning lunch instead of a midmorning snack. Although forks were available, all the children tried to eat with chopsticks. They watched closely the teacher's demonstration and tried to imitate her. Judging by the home reports the teacher received, the Chinese lunch was the highlight of the year in the opinion of both children and parents.

The expression "breaking bread" has implication of sharing, of being on an equal level with those partaking of the meal. Eating is one of the things that the preschool teacher can do in the same way as children; therefore, breaking bread with them can have deep meanings. It seems natural that all adults working with little children would feel a common humanity and be sociable with children at mealtime. Yet, it is not uncommon for teachers in different kinds of preschool programs to merely serve the children, removing themselves from them at mealtimes. Teachers have been seen placing the food on the table (yes, with children's help) and not partaking of it, only feeding the children, and only rarely joining them and engaging in meaningful communication.

In one Head Start program conducted in the rather austere surroundings of an old public school, the teachers, who came from a different community and economic class from those of the children, separated themselves still further from the children by not eating with them. The teachers' reasons included: They were on a diet, they did not like simpler foods served the children, they believed children were better off without adults crowding them, and they said that the children were used to eating by themselves. While the children were eating at the tables, the teachers enjoyed different food nearby, criticizing the children now and then about spills or manners. Eating in that situation was a lonely routine. The teachers missed opportunities to be naturally close to children, to get to know them better, and to share the everyday pleasure of eating which could be done even with some adjustments to the teacher's food preferences and dietary needs.

Eating with children also gives the teacher a chance to be a model for practicing good nutrition. She does not have to talk about vitamins and minerals or urge them to eat something because "it's good for you." Rather, involvement in the partaking of a variety of simple nutritious food attractively presented exposes children to good nutrition and influences their preferences and tastes. For instance, a bowl of fresh raw vegetables can attract the children as they distinguish the circles of carrots, the sticks of celery, the loose leaves of lettuce or spinach, small radishes, and chunks of turnips, perhaps. As a result children are most likely to choose favorite vegetables, express preferences, describe differences, and cultivate tastes. Since they are generally fond of bread, delicious slices spread with honey or butter can be a welcome change from the daily cookies.

Cheese is another wholesome food that should be served. Children can learn that cheese comes in different colors, textures, shapes, and tastes. They can even become interested in the names of cheeses: a whole wheel or a crumbly hunk of Cheddar, a package of smooth sliced American, pieces of delicately soft Munster, etc. Children as well as the teacher could learn much from making cottage cheese from milk. (Be sure to spread on crackers for everyone to enjoy.) Then "cheese comes from milk" will not be a memorized fact, but knowledge gained from experience, that is, "from hand to head."

When later in the year a new student-teacher in that class remarked, "Don't shake the milk when you are carrying it — it might turn to cream"; the children who heard her answered: "Oh, no. Milk turns to cheese after you keep it on the warm window."*

Then the children, with help from their regular teacher, described to the incredulous young lady how milk changed and how they squeezed the curds and used a cheesecloth.

Teachers as well as parents of preschool children need some knowledge of nutrition in relation to children's immediate health and their complete well-being. There are many scientific studies showing effects of nutrition in infancy and early childhood on total health and development (including intellectual development) and indicating the existence of poor nutrition in a large segment of American preschool population. One cure, along with availability of good food, is knowledge and cultivation of good eating.

*From: *Kindergarten: A Year of Learning* by Marguerita Rudolph and Dorothy H. Cohen. Copyright © 1964 by Meredith Publishing Company. By permission of Appleton-Century-Crofts, Educational Division, Meredith Corporation, p. 78.

6 Cooking: Sensory Involvement

Experience with food and eating, even if it is brief and incidental, can lead to actual planned, supervised preparation of edible food. Yes, real cooking for little children results in real learning.

I am aware of commonly voiced objections or questions of teachers and administrators about *danger* from fire, heat, and knives and about children's *incapability* of handling cooking utensils and performing cooking tasks and their short attention span. Objectors also comment on the fact that cooking involves *work* which is too much for playful preschool children and for already *busy teachers* to handle. Some teachers also doubt that they are good enough cooks *themselves* to be able to teach anybody else. To respond to such objections it is necessary to find out what cooking can mean to children.

A teacher, of course, must take the responsibility for avoiding danger and must herself be familiar with handling a stove, hot food, and sharp utensils before helping children use these items. She must *know* the children, which ones are quick and which are cautious. A cooking activity should not be contemplated until teachers and children know each other's interests and ways of working. Then, being aware and respectful of the existence of danger, a teacher has an excellent opportunity to help children recognize danger and observe safety measures: avoidance of contact with fire and steam, process of cooling, use of pot holders, and proper and safe operation of mechanical tools. Learning safety on the job, an interesting job, under secure supervision results in useful knowledge for everybody.

Naturally, three- to six-year-olds cannot be expected to have any competence in cooking without previous experience. However cooking, being real work and generally forbidden to them, arouses instant curiosity. Children quickly get their hands in it, and what they thus learn goes to their heads. The object of cooking in a preschool curriculum is not to train children to be cooks or even mother's helpers, but rather to give them a chance to take part in handling safely a variety of raw materials and simple tools and to carry out an agreed upon responsibility to produce something appreciable. Yes, children are incapable of performing measurements; their concepts of volume and capacity of different containers are hardly reliable! However, they are still fascinated with crude dumping and pouring. A child is likely to put a spoon or hand in a bowl of flour, without any notion of how flour disperses, and to end up with a transformed, thoroughly floured torso! *So do not assume standards* of work in children, but do notice level of interest, nature of physical involvement, and kinds of success. Take advantage of their eagerness and courage to do cooking on a simple but educationally significant level.

As far as a teacher's own skills are concerned, the basic requirements are appreciation of food and of the activity of putting things together, commonsense experience with household utensils, and knowledge of simple cooking procedures, along with awareness of safety. A goal is not to be an instructor in cooking but to be one who learns, who *finds out* with children about physical properties of everyday materials and about the nature of work, and who feels satisfaction from appreciative eaters.

What concrete, appropriate learnings can be expected from cooking activities or even from preparation of foods that do not require cooking (beverages, snacks, salads, desserts)? Cooking provides plenty of opportunities for sensory stimulation and discrimination:

Sight Children can notice great variety of shapes, colors, and patterns and see what happens during the cooking process.

Smell Preschool children have an active sense of smell and will become familiar with many interesting odors, including fruits and spices as well as cooking smells and even objectionable food odors.

Touch This sense may be more involved than others because of young children's proclivity to handle or poke their fingers into everything soft, smooth, sticky, wet, dry, stiff, or moving.

Hearing Cooking sounds are indeed discernible and exciting to children: popping of popcorn, actual snapping of beans, filling or pouring of different liquids, chopping and grinding of vegetables, cracking of nuts, beating of eggs, not to mention slurping!

Taste This sense in young children is a very important and sophisticated means of learning about particular foods and it can lead to intellectual stimulation.

"*What* makes the cookies taste good?" was one child's question which elicited from others analytical comments.

"Raisins make them taste good," one bright-eyed girl replied.

"Plain raisins don't taste the same," said a boy thoughtfully.

"They are sweet—that's why cookies taste good," piped up another child.

"Here is some *sugar*," the teacher offered. "It's sweet. Does it taste like the cookies?"

"No, the cookies are good to bite," another child reasoned.

Other separate ingredients and attributes were mentioned by children while the teacher listened patiently until some showed recognition that the whole is qualitatively different from each part.

Cooking activities provide just as many opportunities for language development as for sensory learning. The sensory stimulation brings out *spontaneous* language, interest in describing, and need for identifying ingredients and utensils ("What's a whisk?"). Children learn about processes: differentiating *sprinkling* and *sifting*, *grating* and *grinding*, *breaking* and *beating*. With fascination and energetic demonstration they use such phrases as "a *pinch* of salt," "time to *punch* the dough," and "*Punch* it!"

Many mathematical operations are integral parts of most cooking activities. There is actual counting of items of ingredients, finished products, needed dishes, and class members present. Fractions are readily used by preschoolers: for example, measuring quantity as they *handle* and learn to differentiate halves and quarters. Such terms as *bigger, smaller, more, not as much, a little bit,* and *enough* are immediately put to use. There are opportunities for engaging in mathematical predictions: "The bag of sugar won't fit into this can." "Maybe we can have two cupcakes a piece" (a response after counting the cakes and counting children). There are times when they become aware of diminishing or increasing volume and differentiation of sizes. The relation of volume to weight challenges and even startles children; a whole potful of raw spinach is expected to be heavier than just a cupful of raw rice!

Although young children may be slow in grasping the concept of time, they still frequently encounter *time* during cooking experiences. They become involved in "watching the time" when something is in the oven and "waiting" till something is cooled. They feel the urgency of serving the risen popovers "quickly" before they fall. When something is to be eaten the "next day," they seldom forget, although in this instance there may be confusion about the transformation of "the next day" into "today." In one class the three- to four-year-olds were understandably vague about the days of the week, but seemed to refer to Friday correctly. *Friday was the assigned cooking day.*

Cooking experiences lead to another significant area of learning: noticing and trying to understand *change.* Children see changing of liquids into solids (as with Jell-O or custard), solids into liquids (melted chocolate). They see a "holdable" solid apple changed into a sticky mass that can only be picked up with a spoon; a shapely banana, into a loose, runny substance; and hard yellow popcorn, into soft white puffs. In fact, the constant changes in color, texture, consistency, and taste from cooking (though hardly noticed and usually taken for granted by grownups) are noticed with interest by children.

"Where is the sugar lump that was dropped in the cup?" asked a child who did not know.

"It was dissolved," the teacher commented matter-of-factly.

"Dissolved! You don't see it anymore, it *disappeared,*" the child may have concluded.

When a child realizes that he is the one who can affect changes with his own hands, he makes a very important discovery. He can scoop some sugar and pour it and stir it with a wooden spoon; he can make that sour applesauce taste as sweet as he likes it.

"It looks too pale!" he may say.

"All right then, stir in some red jelly and you have pink apple sauce," the teacher may suggest. "You did it!"

A teacher may use this dramatic aspect of change to expand awareness and stimulate inquiry. What kind of things dissolve? What happens to them? Can you retrieve something that has been dissolved?

How does such learning take place in spontaneous concrete activities in a classroom full of preschoolers? Naturally, start with something simple that takes short preparation time and uses few ingredients and easy, familiar utensils. Ask no more than three or four children to work together. Prepare something that many children like.

When Mrs. Bender suggested bringing lemonade for her daughter's class birthday party, the teacher persuaded the mother to supply real lemons so that the children could take part in making it. When the teacher told them "the news," their response showed that they liked lemonade, and that the idea of making anything was exciting. At this time the teacher felt confident that they were ready for the task. Their curious questions: "Will it be real lemonade?" (as opposed to make-believe) and "How do you make lemonade?" indicated that there was much the children did not know. Mrs. Bender caught the children's curiosity and became intrigued by the project.

"I am looking forward to coming!" she said.

The teacher was already prepared and organized for the lemonade experience when she greeted the children that day. She had cleared a large table where all the ingredients were now on one end and a row of utensils on the other. She wore an apron with a hand towel attached. The teacher appointed four workers, promising to call others later if any one dropped out.

"We have to work with clean hands," the teacher said, washing her own in front of the children.

Behaving differently than at other hand-washing times, the children complied readily. Now they were eager to get their still wet hands into everything, but this situation required teacher control. Her plan was to make the activity meaningful, enjoyable, *and* successful. She did not hesitate to frustrate the impulses of the four-year-old children; she believed they could wait, for they *knew* the teacher had something good for them.

"Before we start working, let's see what we have," she said.

Then the children, in their own way, examined the ingredients:

the line of eight lemons, the open canister with sugar and a measuring scoop, a large pitcher of plain water, and a small jar of preserved cherries. They counted and fingered and smelled the lemons; they pinched and licked the sugar (again and again). Using a paper cup they hesitantly touched and drank the water, making sure it was water. They enjoyed tasting a portion of the cherries, too. How all those ingredients were going to be combined to make lemonade was certainly not clear to the children even after the teacher answered their questions. With her full attention, they inspected the utensils: the sharp knife that was to be used only by the teacher on a cutting board, the three different hand squeezers, a strainer with a spoon, and a mixing bowl with a wooden mixing spoon.

"So many tools!" one child exclaimed and promptly proceeded to count the items as others joined him.

The teacher waited patiently until the counting ended. Then the children watched and waited patiently while she cut the lemons in half, which inspired more counting as well as comments on the design of the cross section of the lemon and the appearance of seeds.

Something happened then that the teacher had not anticipated. One child wanted to eat a piece of plain lemon. The teacher thought it would be a good experience for *comparison* with the taste of the finished lemonade, so she sliced off slivers for the children and herself. This proved to be unexpected *fun* as all watched each other's (and the teacher's) contorted faces. This merriment brought responses from the other adults and children.

Finally, the work proper began. First, all the juice was squeezed out of the lemons. The four children really exerted themselves in pressing and twisting, noticeably improving their techniques and result as they worked. The teacher, working along with them, noticed that Bobby who often boasted of his muscle strength in "beating somebody up," was using his real strength differently. After they helped strain the juice into the bowl, each of the four children poured in a measure of sugar and some water. The most fascinating operation was *stirring* each item added and causing splashing.

The teacher directed each step, "No, don't put any more water. I'd better taste it now."

She deliberately dramatized this step, conveying that tasting was a *critical* activity, different from plain eating or drinking. The children watched her serious judging expression and with evident curiosity, waited for the verdict. All that attention from the children was flattering to the teacher and tempted her to prolong the suspense, but she managed to keep her attention on the project as a whole. She showed her verdict with an agreeable facial expression.

"The lemonade tastes delicious *to me!*" she said. To give the children a chance to be critical, too, she then added, "One of you should taste it, to see if it needs anything."

Each one wanted to "do tasting," but time was important now, and the teacher asked the boy with muscle power to exercise his critical power for a change.

"It's a little sour to me," he said thoughtfully.

"What should you do about it?" the teacher asked.

None of the four-year-olds had the answer. Although each of them had dumped sugar into the liquid, apparently it was beyond them to deduct that since sugar is in itself sweet, you must add it to improve the sour taste of the lemonade. The teacher then simply advised Bobby to add a scoop of sugar, stir till dissolved, and *taste again.* This was suspenseful for everybody. What a joyful expression Bobby's face had, joyful from having just learned something.

"It worked!" he exclaimed. "The sugar made it taste sweet."

Knowing this child, the teacher sensed his personal pleasure from having made the change in the taste of the lemonade.

Next, other children put cherry juice with cherries into the bowl, stirred the mixture, and observed the change in color.

"The cherry juice made it a little pink," they noted.

Perhaps the children's experience with color mixture in painting made them anticipate and notice this change.

Transferring the lemonade with a cup from the bowl into the pitcher and counting the cupfuls were much more fascinating to the children than any adult could anticipate. The four children took turns and kept track of the turns mathematically: "I am second, you are third."

Not having a *strict lesson* plan, the teacher was still responsible for following safety procedures, for timing, and for control of activities and children, as well as being attuned to their responses. What a vast amount of learning occurred during the practical 45-minute task of making lemonade! This was learning that could be correctly described as sensory, intellectual, motor, verbal, and social.

Other simple kinds of cooking are similar in scope to making lemonade. Jell-O, for instance, involves measuring, stirring carefully, observing dissolving and change of color, transferring liquid or solid from bowl to individual serving dishes, estimating quantity, and counting portions. The process could be elaborated on by using two flavors, adding fruits, or using fruit juice instead of water.

Even a simpler food, buttered bread, is difficult but interesting for preschool children to prepare. They may have little opportunity to do it at home. Buttering bread requires coordination with which preschoolers struggle: holding bread with one hand, spreading it with the other, and exerting limited pressure. The difficulty in making a sandwich comes not only in applying or distributing the right amount of substance, but also in making the two parts *fit*. It takes much patience — patience which children have, but which adults usually do not.

An adult prefers saying, "Let me finish it." or "Let me do it for you this time."

There is no precise distinction between simple and more advanced cooking. It probably depends upon the teacher's skill and confidence as well as upon the children's experiences. For instance, popovers require only four ingredients (flour, salt, eggs, and milk) and no careful combining of each item. Just dumping and sloshing everything together seems to be the appropriate procedure. The only thing that could be called difficult is thorough greasing and filling of the pans, an activity all children like to do. Any adult can do the temperature setting of the oven and timing. Adults seem to be most worried about having such a glamorous product "come out right." To banish such fear, the teacher should bake some popovers herself first so that she will be familiar with the process and the result. Then in the classroom she can focus on the experience and learning of the children and not be concerned with her idea of success.

Although success is an aim in cooking, failure can be impressive and important. My experience in a baking failure involving an older nursery school class served as an unforgettable lesson. In spite of careful accounting for the various dry ingredients and for the liquids and the flavorings for an orange cake, something was forgotten. At the height of everybody's expectation of enjoying the cake, the first bite brought disappointment. The cake wasn't sweet enough! Half of the sugar had been forgotten. What drama, and what humor—especially as recalled later! Were children discouraged?

"Let's make another cake," a child suggested right away.

"And don't forget the sugar!" became a theme song for subsequent cooking sessions. "Check off the ingredients before we are through" became the teacher's formula, and the children knew exactly what she meant.

Besides the dramatic attraction of many cooking projects, there is also an element of adventure. A teacher may not be entirely sure what is going to happen, and children may engage in speculations: "Maybe we'll have enough pancakes for the whole school?" "Maybe for the whole world!" While watching salt and spices being added to the soup, they may pronounce "Look! They are putting poison in." Cooking is adventurous because it results in something new to be shared by all. When the result is a recognized success, the self-satisfaction of the participants is enormous!

When complicated dishes are made, the necessary conditions are good timing so that the teacher does not feel harassed and adult help in the classroom so that children who are not involved in cooking can be adequately supervised. If children's activities and questions lead the teacher to decide that vegetable soup would be most interesting to make in class, she has to estimate the time for preparation as well as the time for cooking and eating. Her involvement with a special project affects other activities and routines. Perhaps short sessions are needed: a session to do the *preparation* of vegetables on one day and the cooking proper on the next. If baking a cake is planned, dry ingredients could be sifted, measured, and mixed one day; liquids added and combined the next.

Since the value of the cooking experience comes from the children's full involvement, there should not be too many on one operation. Otherwise the teacher will be busy admonishing children, expediting division of labor, or demonstrating and expecting them to learn by just watching. Depending upon the children and the teacher, two to six members can be a comfortable work crew. The problem that presents itself then is proper provision for those who may be involved in other activities. In such situations a second adult is indispensable, whether she is a trained assistant, a practical aide, a willing volunteer, or a helpful mother. Perhaps it is this second person who has the interest and patience to be in charge of a cooking project while the teacher takes care of the rest of the class. In either case the children's needs will not be over-looked.

When supervision of work crew members and timing is handled smoothly, the teacher can venture into "advanced" cooking. She can plan to do it with the children as a result of particular experience or evident interest. Watching a hand of green bananas turn ripe and yellow, the children would very likely be intrigued by doing something else with the bananas besides eating them plain, for example, baking a banana cake or banana bread. If it is assumed that the children have already handled a sifter, have used measuring devices, have broken eggs, and have poured or spooned and scraped batter, the work could proceed with a tolerable amount of messing and a maximum of exciting learning. The teacher can also be assured of finding out something new about problems, pleasures, and particular children. There can be a brief, pertinent planning discussion between the group of children and adults regarding *what* the needed ingredients are, *where* to get them, *when* the work will take place, *who* the workers will be, and *how* big the cake will have to be. Being in on planning gives all the children a sense of participation as well as of pride and importance. The planning discussion might well include others than the signed-up crew.

Here is a scene from a banana cake project. When the work started, the children looked over the familiar ingredients and found one they did not know—*baking soda*. They had assumed *soda* would be in a bottle. Some were curious enough to promptly taste it and their reaction discouraged others from doing the same, yet challenged a few to "let me taste." Among the utensils the masher for the bananas was especially attractive, and the children predicted that the mashed banana would be soft and fluffy. The children worked simultaneously, two on each operation of sifting the flour, beating the eggs, creaming the shortening, and mashing the bananas. The latter proved most surprising because of the extracted liquid and the visibility of curious black specks of seeds. Aware of how discerning children were, the teacher called their attention to the color of the ingredients.

"Everything is white!" they said, enumerating seven white ingredients.

Children who were beating the eggs added, "But eggs are a little bit yellow."

"Well, what color will the banana cake be?" the teacher queried.

"White," the children predicted.

"We'll see . . ." the teacher said mysteriously when the children asked her opinion.

The pervasive, appetizing aroma of a cake in the oven, the suspense of the banana cake's slow baking, and the speculation about its color contributed to an atmosphere of excitement and adventure. The surprisingly darkish banana cake was acclaimed "delicious."

It is important for the teacher to realize that, although no more than a fourth of a group may be actively involved in the cooking task, others are aware, curious, and watchful and should have a chance to ask questions, appreciate the result, and in general receive considerable stimulation from the project. They too feel part of the exciting happening, especially baking a cake for a particular occasion.

When the children learned that their parents were coming to an evening meeting in their classroom, they showed great enthusiasm for baking a cake.

"We have to make two cakes," five-year-old Larry calculated.

The teacher thought Larry was being unusually mathematical and was estimating the capacity of adult eaters. But that was not the case!

"One for us," he qualified, "and one for the mommies and daddies."

And thus two days were spent in cake baking, with all the children singing praises of themselves at school and at home.

The reader may conclude that cooking should dominate the curriculum, and that all cooking projects should consist of making glamorous or surprising dishes or should entail scientific discoveries. Only a teacher with special interest (and easily available helping adults) would plan cooking as often as once a week! It would be more realistic to plan cooking projects once in two weeks or less frequently, but regularly, so that the meaning of the experience can be assessed. The teacher could probably see the value of it over a period of a few sessions when she sees the reaction of children, parents, and colleagues.

As to the selection of food to cook—children's interest is the best criterion, as shown in the following situation.

A class of four- to seven-year-old children had an opportunity to harvest onions from a nearby farm. All the children were indeed interested not only in cooking them, but also, to the surprise of the adults, in eating buttered boiled onions! In that case it was the manual labor of harvesting that influenced the children's attitude and appetite. Other plain vegetables could be used in similar activities.

Some ordinary foods are interesting to prepare because they allow the children to use tools and produce transformations, as happen in mashing potatoes and making cracker crumbs. Another ordinary food that can be of great interest to prepare is cinnamon toast. The preparation entails *spreading* melted or softened butter on toast, *shaking* on sugar to cover the surface, *sprinkling* cinnamon, and seeing it melt into the butter. Distinguishing all these actions is a work of the hands, the senses, and the mind.

There is no limit to what any teacher using *her own ideas* and resourcefulness can do to have safe, appropriate, and pleasurable cooking experiences.

7 Seeds and Plants; Flowers and Fruits

Since plants or parts of plants can be found practically anywhere, it is easy for children and adults—if they look—to see the prevalence and variety of plant life around them irrespective of location, climate, or season of the year. What a natural subject for early childhood education nature and plants are! Plants in pots on sunny windows, flowering shrubs in parks and gardens, sturdy trees to tie a swing on, falling petals, climbing vines, and tangled roots attract children's attention. The attention may be passive and passing, or it may lead to further contact, depending upon the teacher's sensitivity to children's interest.

Coming upon growing things accidentally can arouse a great deal of curiosity. A small dark seed attached to a tiny white parachute floating through the air sparks the query: "Where did it come from?" Since milkweed is quite a common plant, it may be possible to obtain the ripe, dry, conical milkweed pod packed with thousands of little seeds, capable of opening and parachuting. A teacher may find something even more common like a bumpy, pale sprout on a brown potato inside a paper bag. Questions are certain to include: "What's happening to the potato?" Keeping track of the changes in the sprouts stimulates more interest and questions from children. (When collecting and using seeds, teachers should be aware that some are poisonous.)

A shiny brown locust seed detaches itself from the pod which falls from the tree. "Can this seed grow?" the children ask. It would be interesting for them to germinate the tiny seed and locate its parent, the full-size tree!

In contrast with the smallness of a seed, the gigantic dimensions of only part of a plant can provide significant encounters for preschool children. After a flash storm a class of young children went to see an uprooted tree. The tree was ten feet in diameter, with a mass of tangled roots defying description. However, the most powerful attribute of the tree, and of immediate meaning to the children, was its crushing weight. The tree had fallen on three parked cars, completely demolishing one of them. A fallen giant indeed. "*Awful* big" as a child said!

The teacher need not have knowledge of botany, but rather have a spirit of inquiry and response to children's curiosity so that she can help them notice more and try to see relationships. Preschool children picking up acorns from the ground may assume that the acorns originated on the ground. Only after craning their necks and identifying the cluster of acorns among the oak leaves do they think that the acorns on the oak tree are related to those on the ground.

In a school in an eastern suburb a tremendous profusion of winged seeds covers the playground right under a spreading maple. However, it takes four-year-old George days to make the observation: "They come from this tree! I see them falling." Only after considerable watching is he able to make the mathematical connection: a few falling seeds and a few more and as they keep falling become a huge pile. This is not just simple arithmetic. The difference between "a few" and "a lot" is not only in numbers but also in appearance. A few seeds, and a few more, and . . . look what happens. An accumulation! An immeasurable quantity! You cannot say a number for it. Nature's productions are far from simple, both in quantity and in function, and young children form misconceptions very easily.

When small potatoes were actually picked off the stringy roots of a potato plant in a deep window box in class, the children were awed by the success of their growing plant and especially by the edible potatoes. The first thing that one child did when he got home was to dig up a grapefruit plant, hoping of course to pick edible grapefruit from the roots of the plant.

Handling a wide variety of plants in school can extend children's experiences with nature and stimulate activities and projects that involve scientific, artistic, and social learning. What the teacher needs in this area is not a unit of study for the children but a workable plan for her own learning about the immediate natural environment. Also, she must think of appropriate outdoor activities for children for the different seasons, and she must find out about their homes as possible resources. She can help children be more aware not only of existence of plant life, but also of the usefulness of plants to people. Recognition that plants provide one source of food can give children some down-to-earth values and appreciation of the plant-supporting earth. It provides them with a reason for celebrating Earth Day and discovering what the earth does for them and what they might do to protect it.

When the preschool program includes activities involving food, children have an opportunity to regard plants as food. Different colors and sizes of ripe fruits and berries, different kinds of juicy edible leaves, and a variety of other vegetables made available to children over a period of time result in practical knowledge. Knowledge touched with imagination captures the interest of a young child. Unwrap a corn cob and discover how each kernel is attached. Open a sealed pea pod and watch how the peas scatter! These vivid experiences help children *know* that each vegetable has its own covering, color, and curious shape.

Access to a real garden, an orchard, or a pasture with grazing animals naturally gives children most direct knowledge of growing plants as food. However, visiting and obtaining fresh products from nearby fruit and vegetable markets with attractive, colorful displays should not be overlooked.

Usefulness and cultivation of plants as nourishment for people and animals can be presented to young children on a personal level and readily understood in any environment. Usefulness of plants such as wood for construction is more complicated. Tree products (boards, lumber, wood) are abstractions and are not the same as a tree to a child, and he may not relate them unless he sees the process. However, visiting a lumber yard, a furniture factory, a neighborhood building construction, or a place where baskets are made enables him to see the raw material and to get a notion of the great usefulness of wood.

Usefulness of trees for shade in the summer is more easily understood. Yet the teacher should not take shade trees for granted. Which trees provide shade? Is it the height or the width of a tree that is important? There are many questions to ask and answers to explore.

What kind of learning comes from trees besides the reality and poetry of trees? Trees serve and shelter man. Can man in turn protect them?

If a school has an indoor or outdoor fireplace or working wood stove and a place to gather firewood, a group of preschool children with a responsive teacher can have a great experience. Picking up and breaking up branches, sticks, and bark, taking precautions in making a fire, getting a notion of wood as a source of fuel, and seeing the startling change of wood to coal and ashes are unforgettable activities.

Appreciating plants for their decoration and beauty is a continuous, ongoing experience. The teacher may provide indoor plants that can be cared for and attended by the children. She may bring bouquets of fresh flowers to class. As a result children may often bring in fragrant plants from their parents' gardens. Colorful boughs of leaves in the fall or a winter gathering of stalks and nonpoisonous pods should not be forgotten. When a teacher *shares* her sense of beauty in these ways, it comes across to the children. They may not talk about the beauty they perceive, which is perfectly understandable. Beauty is a subjective and subtle feeling; yet we know it is real.

These experiences with nature may motivate some children to express their feelings about it in a variety of art activities: painting, molding, and constructing something esthetic with shapes, colors, and textures. Sometimes a particular book evokes or heightens with words and pictures an esthetic experience with nature.

Having plants in the classroom could mean establishing at some time a true laboratory where preschool children can start a planting project. In such a setting they can observe changes in development of a sprout and can see again and again transformation of a small dry seed into an expanding, growing, living plant or transformation of a closed green bud into soft, open, purple petals. Children can put chunky carrot tops in a dish with no water and over a few days observe that the tops become dry and shriveled up. They can experiment with drowning these same carrot tops with water and note that they soon rot. Children may put some carrot tops in a dish with water and a few pebbles on the bottom, and in a few days observe a green garden growing taller and taller above while rooting below. Similarly, yet differently, a sweet potato, too, develops an intricate system of threadlike roots, and the sprouts grow into beautiful leafy vines. The sweet potato will continue to grow and become a decoration in the classroom, even a conversation piece, but by no means idle conversation.

One teacher, regarding her classroom as a laboratory for the children and herself, put a few onions on the table one day just to see what the children would do with them. Characteristically, the children who noticed the onions stopped to touch, to handle, to scrape the papery "skin," to play with the onions, and to smell them repeatedly. Overcome by tears, but still playful, one of them finally concluded: "Onions make your *eyes* cry." No one taught this child such truth; she learned it from her own senses and her own helping hand while investigating raw material and making free comments. Her comment was well understood by the other blinking, laughing children. To the teacher it showed the depth and aptness of a child's expression.

Children everywhere at any age like digging in the soil, and nothing could be more welcome in a class than a container of planting soil. Some preliminary playful (even though controlled) handling of the soil itself is a must before actual planting or transplanting takes place. This activity enables children to investigate texture, moisture, and even temperature of soil before they transfer it into a flowerpot, window box, or improvised used cartons of appropriate dimensions. The seeds to be planted must also be inspected and handled by the curious children in their own way. It is very interesting to have a good look at this seed which is going to be hidden in the soil and which will change to become a plant. The *process of planting* is fascinating play.

The teacher should not try to instruct children beyond conveying that the plant needs soil, sun, air, and water. It is certainly difficult to understand how a tiny flat speck of a seed contains the potential of a full live plant that has roots, flowers, and its own seeds. Therefore, when something is planted in soil, some children invariably want to dig up the seed to *see* what happened to it the next day. It is worthwhile to keep a special pot for a child to try to peek at the mystery. A transparent plastic or glass container with seeds and moist absorbent paper provides a good view of germination.

Aliveness of a plant is manifested by changes in growth and need for nourishment, both analogous to aspects of human aliveness. Another consideration of the analogy of living plants to humans, which intrigues children, is the awareness that plants get sick. A tree infested with tent caterpillars and losing foilage is a graphic sight of such sickness. A medicated, tarred tree trunk may be present in some neighborhoods, and children may have an opportunity to see a tree surgeon at work. Children can easily distinguish blights on vegetables and fruits which can be termed unhealthy. They may be interested in the names of plant diseases; for instance, a repugnant dark growth on top of kernels of corn on the cob is called *smut*. What a good name for a disease!

Change of seasons bringing change in plants is dramatically manifested in the fall wherever deciduous trees grow. Children always notice change of color and the movement of windblown falling leaves. Again, there are immeasurable quantities—armfuls, masses, mounds and "mountains" for children to play in, to feel, to think about.

As in other experiences that lead to learning, the preschool teacher should not be strictly scientific with naming, giving causes of natural phenomena, or quizzing children. Instead, she should just be *herself* appreciative of nature and try to share in the children's activities and learning.

Although *grow* is a well-known word to young children, because they hear it often as it applies to them personally, it usually suggests only getting bigger.

When three-year-old Ann asked what would happen to a nut that was not eaten, she was told it would be planted.

"Why?" she asked.

"So it will grow," the teacher replied. "The nut is a seed."

Ann apparently thought this over and concluded: "Then it will be a big nut."

How *logical* this is from her point of view. How would she know that growth is changing and taking in and giving out, that growth is not only the same thing getting bigger but also becoming something else. It takes experience and complicated learning to know *all that*, the reader might rightly think. Yet, a laboratory in which children may play, watch, and work with plants and seeds and draw their own conclusions stimulates them to develop concepts of growth.

All this intellectually significant work with plants may seem to be extra educational responsibility, perhaps a burden, for a teacher. She can temper this responsibility by making use of other adults and resources. Some parents may have, for example, a cultivated garden, a small plot, or a sunny window with profuse begonia blossoms or bright geraniums. The children might visit such a parent and bring a plant back for the room. In one school the custodian spoke of his weekend trips to a brother's apple orchard and how he had harvested apples there. So, the custodian was invited to be a special honored guest (bringing a basket of apples) of the city children. They talked with him about apple growing and picking and also about the care of the trees. They got a vivid glimpse of farm life and labor and the usefulness of trees to needy humans.

Since it is the human contact that is so important and influential in all young children's learning, the more outside people who share their planting experiences with children and the teacher, the better and more important learning becomes.

Not long ago I had occasion to visit a child care center in a city during the month of June. Having discovered daisies in an abandoned field near home, I gathered a bouquet to bring to the city children. I joined a circle of three-year-olds seated on the floor and showed them the lovely white daisies.

"Flower," one child after another uttered softly.

Then the children gained courage: "I want one," echoed through the group. There were enough flowers, and each child held a daisy happily in his hand, looking it over.

"Take it to my mommy" was the next expression of interest.

"Yes, when you go home you will take the flower to Mommy," I told the children. "But now, put the flower in water here, so that it will stay fresh."

Trustingly the children complied. Each walked over to the bowl of water on the table and thrust the flower, head down, into the water. *Logically,* putting a *flower* in water meant putting the blossom part in water, not the stem! These three-year-olds had not had experience with keeping cut flowers. They looked surprised when the amused teacher righted all the daisies.

How clearly children show their naivety, their responsiveness to what is offered them, their trust in adults, and their readiness for *personal* experiences with materials — in this case a flower to hold, to behold, and to "take to Mommy."

8 Transportation: Everything Goes

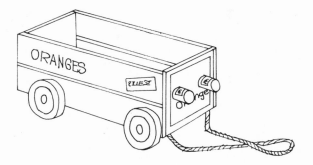

The reader may wonder why transportation is a subject for early childhood education. The answer is that young children themselves are full of action and motion and they are always "on the go." They respond readily to anything that moves. A most popular toy for children (with the possible exception of dolls) is a transportation toy. In preschool establishments there are usually some transportation toys, such as cars, trucks, boats, planes, wagons, and tricycles. It is universally accepted that such items are appealing and meaningful to children and meet a preschool educational need.

Children as young as two years are keen observers of transportation in their lives. Anyone who drives a car with a preschooler as a passenger can attest to the fact that a child quickly familiarizes himself with all visible parts of the vehicle, all actions and gestures of the operator, as well as with the sounds and motions (and imaginary sensations) of the car. Although young children's sense of direction is not totally reliable since they can get lost easily in a store or even near home, they often show uncanny awareness of correct turns and locations during transportation. School bus drivers as well as parents find that children watch and remember how to get not only to their own home, but also to other children's houses. Let the driver make a wrong turn and invariably some children notice it! Direction is an aspect of transportation, and young children are ready for practice in finding direction.

Children are vitally interested in their own immediate transportation, and they quickly develop an interest in it in general. They are fascinated by travel on land, in water, in the air, underground, and in outer space. In the early years of aviation one heard many anecdotes about little ones identifying different types of aircraft. A newspaper cartoon, alluding to the dominance of popular interest in air travel, showed a child pointing to a bird in flight and saying, "What kind of a plane is that, daddy?" What dominates the interest of society is of concern to children. Preschool children of today can often identify jets, spaceships, and lunar vehicles as well. Obviously they are not ready for scientific information or technical explanations of modern transport. Characteristically young children *react* to the essential aspects of their culture though they may not actually *understand* what is happening. They show this reaction in their intense regard for transportation.

In the first two weeks of a summer kindergarten near an Arizona Indian reservation the Indian children did not talk much, especially to the non-Indian teacher. Douglas, though alert and active, was a child of few words until something of major importance happened at home. It was the arrival of a new pickup truck. He had something to say then about the pickup truck, and the expression of enthusiasm and humor in his face showed the importance of that truck. The teacher who was native to the community explained: "All of the kids think their pickup trucks are the greatest."

In making plans for programs and materials the preschool teacher needs first to discover what interests the children most. As she does this, she soon observes that transportation does interest young children. How can she take advantage of this interest to lead children to related activities and learning? Should she simply let them play in their own ways with sturdy, safe transportation toys and leave learning to the children themselves? These are crucial questions. When children are involved in *what they want to do*, the teacher can see *what they want to learn*. Then she can help them learn *what they need to know*.

When a child shows a persistent strong interest, he can effectively use the teacher's guidance in problem solving during that activity, in further understanding what he is handling, and in observing safety procedures. A broken wheel is quickly diagnosed by a child when motion of a toy truck is impeded. The same child may not understand why an empty wagon moves easily and a loaded one makes him huff and puff as he pulls it. The teacher has an opportunity to enlarge children's awareness of power required in all transportation. She does this without intrusion into their play. She can show them her recognition of their body power! After children run and race, they are glad to hear that they have leg and foot power. With this power they have "go" and can get places. A child thus learns about his own body power as well as about transportation. He learns to assess such power when he says: "*Both* of us will pull — it will be faster."

Being familiar with pulling enables children to appreciate greater pull power of horses. It is quite impressive to children (and adults) to become acquainted with a working farm horse, to see him pull a load, and to see him rest and eat.

"He has big teeth. The horse has to eat a lot to be strong," observed a child on a class visit to an agricultural high school. He was speaking from his own experience because he had heard frequently the admonition: "Eat, so you'll be strong." His comment occasioned intelligent, though brief, discussion of the food horses eat and of the need for food to supply energy. Enjoying the children's close attention, the student guide pointed to a tractor and said, "She won't run without food either." Several four-year-olds knew that the tractor had a motor. The analogy of gas fuel for the motor and food fuel for the animal was enjoyed by the children, who can easily look at inanimate objects as animate.

Wheels are fascinating to children of all ages. Interest in different aspects of transportation can lead children (with the teacher's help) to focus on wheels. They are familiar with wheels from experiences with tricycles, wheelbarrows, cars, and other kinds of vehicles. Children can actually discover the advantage of a wheel simply and convincingly by pulling a box with a load of objects and then rolling a wheeled vehicle containing the same load.

Today's children readily distinguish different motor vehicles they see, not only the ones in which they ride. One lady was astonished to hear her grandson, not yet three, tell her of the family's "wed volkswagen." How could he say such a difficult word when he is still at the stage of using the *w* sound for an r sound? The explanation lies not in the child's linguistic precocity but in his preoccupation with driving. At home he converted any round object into a "steering wheel" and "drove" it noisily all day long it seemed! Children in nursery school also frequently become preoccupied with steering wheels in the same way.

Children notice different kinds and sizes of cars, buses, and delivery trucks that may come to the school or home. They like to talk about them, share observations, and ask questions. This interest applies to air transportation too. Children are aware of the observable reality of flight and the tangible features of aircraft. They struggle to understand the relation of perceivable size to distance. Seeing preparation for a flight such as provision of fuel, inspection of particular working parts, and essential service to passengers gives them practical knowledge.

In becoming more aware of transportation power, whether human muscle power, or horsepower, or motor power, children also learn about the direction, the control, and the *stop* aspects of travel. They realize that with the "go" there is an inevitable appropriate "stop."

This overall appeal of travel in preschool learning requires that provisions be made to further children's knowledge and acquaintance with transportation. First, there is direct experience with real cars, planes, and boats and the people who operate them. Different kinds of service trucks coming to the school are most interesting for children to climb inside and inspect. Working adults are usually responsive and cooperative when told that they can assist with the children's education, but they must be invited ahead of time.

One of the most exciting visitors a nursery school had was the neighborhood traffic policeman. The children spontaneously asked him practical questions about traffic! Before leaving, the policeman told them, "I bet you know traffic rules better than some grown-ups!"

There may be garages, airports, or docks near enough to visit so that children can make firsthand observations. Before taking them to such a place, the teacher would need to go there first alone in order to see if it is safe and accessible for children and to meet persons in charge.

People in any aspect of transportation are invariably as important as machinery. When a group of children returned to class after going inside a docked oil tanker, they enumerated every feature of the tanker and told how the oil *trucks* were filled with oil from the tankers. But what seemed to be especially worth talking about was the sight of the crew eating lunch. The children seemed to have a fresh awareness that the big, heavy boat with all its working parts had working *people* who not only operated the boat, but also *lived* on it and ate piles of mashed potatoes and hamburgers.

The same group of children showed tremendous interest in trains, although many of them had not been on one. There was a railroad station in the suburb where they lived, and they had seen local trains pulling in or pulling out and express trains whizzing by. But what mattered most was the fact that every child had either a commuting father or a relative who had to be met at the station. The teacher, therefore, was convinced that a real train trip to the next town would be indeed meaningful to these four-year-olds. She felt the activity would be worth the trouble of arranging for the best time, collecting money for each child to have a ticket, and planning a convenient way of returning. The children might have seen the ticket office, the waiting room, and the platform before, but this time it was *their* trip. They had their tickets and were waiting to board the train. (An adult must really watch a child to see how exciting and urgent the sound and sensation of an approaching train can be.) Their excitement continued as they boarded, settled in strange seats, had their tickets punched, noticed the passing scenes and structures, speculated on speed, anticipated a stop, got out and watched other passengers getting off and new ones getting on, then heard the conductor call out "All Aboard!" and heard the doors close, and felt the train in motion. All this was experienced through the senses by each child as a *whole* person. The teacher was right! This activity proved to be "the greatest event of the school year," in the opinion of the teachers and the parents as well as of the children. Following that trip the children played out all the details of train travel.

Since another class train trip was too complicated to plan, the teacher settled for a second-best one. The group went to the station very near the school to see a train from the city pull in, discharge passengers, and take on others. For this trip the teacher and children had to know the time and watch the clock, and consider caution, safety, and discipline. At the station they enjoyed the suspense of a train's arrival and the friendly hand waving of the engineer. That trip had its own rewards. It elicited keen observation and good conversation from the children.

In thinking of the fascination of trains for young children, I recall an incident during the New York World's Fair in the sixties. While waiting for a train to the Fair, a suburban mother tried to inform her two children, four to six years of age, where they were going and what they would see. But they were obviously more attentive to inspecting the platform and the tracks, pointing to where the train would soon be visible, putting their hands on the ears in anticipation of loud noise, and then jumping for joy when the train became visible. In reply to a stranger's question, "Where are you all going?" both children replied, "On the train!" Children's enthusiasm for trains seems the same in different parts of our own and other lands.

It is important for children not only to have direct experiences with travel and opportunity at the same time to ask questions and to talk about it on their own level and with adults, but also to *play* transportation. Through dramatic, imaginative, spontaneous play children express interest and ideas, pursue knowledge, and conceptualize problems. It is desirable to have a *real* old car, boat, or buggy made stationary on the playground. The vehicle must be safe for children to use freely, to get in and out of, to manipulate, to manage, and to add other parts such as ropes or boards. The condition of safety can never be taken for granted as far as young children are concerned. When daily inspection is done by a grown-up with children, it brings in important realistic learning about transportation: serious checking of the vehicle to ensure safe use. Children actually give such a task responsible attention. Some days the inspection may turn into dramatic play. At other times they may find extraneous clutter which endangers seating or a rip in the car upholstery requiring immediate patching or secure covering. Objects that tend to prevent safe entrance may need to be placed elsewhere. Unexpected animal inhabitants may need to be removed. Such activity, though interesting itself, can teach respect for safety and enable children to feel free to put the real vehicle to imaginative use.

Imaginative play cannot be taken for granted, and the children involved cannot be left entirely alone by the teacher. If she rushes in only when there is trouble, results may indicate bad judgment. Even geographic arguments ("Isn't Chicago farther than Africa?") require attention before they are settled. A teacher who keeps an eye on the play can ascertain the need for particular additional props such as a seat, a gangplank, a side-view mirror, or a rope with an anchor. A tool box with appropriate and safe-to-use items is a *must* for any vehicle and is usually well guarded by children. A pail for "bailing" out the boat is an item all children will want to have available.

Another prop needed is a real or improvised hat for a chauffer, a service station attendant, or a captain; several different types may be needed. Wearing an appropriate hat seems to be a magic ingredient in playing a successful role.

Realistic pictures of various kinds of transportation can enable dramatic play to become more educational and enjoyable. These can be cut from local newspapers or national magazines to which teachers and parents subscribe. Pictures can also be obtained from railway or airline offices, industrial publicity departments, and travel bureaus. The teacher may also obtain slides or filmstrips that are informative and stimulating to preschool children who already have had firsthand experiences, who can differentiate the real from the pictorial, and who are ready to understand various details. It is experience along with play which provides the basis or background that enables children to handle specific knowledge of simple technical matters of transportation and to gain an appreciation of human skills and social values which are graphically and artistically shown in good pictures.

Preschool children can also get a perspective of transportation by having a hand in construction of items. Some child will want to make "a car" with whatever objects (such as bottle caps) that suggest wheels. No matter how crude the hand-propelled "car" is, other children will want to make one, too. Here, depending upon the child's interest and skills, a teacher can help him relate construction to use, discover kinds of attachments which enable the wheels to roll, and decide what other parts that his car may need and that he can construct. A child's spontaneous crossing of two narrow pieces of wood which he promptly calls an "airplane" is then held high in his hand while he whirls about making realistic sounds of contemporary aircraft. That bit of construction of a symbol of a plane *puts him in touch with the reality of the plane and stimulates his imagination.*

Children can also take part in construction of vehicles that are more practical and durable than the small toy ones. For example, a sturdy wooden box and wheels from an old baby carriage or a tricycle (found in junk shops or junkyards) provide enough materials for a crude but satisfactory usable wagon which an adult with only rudimentary construction skills can make. Children can share their ideas about construction and do such work as sanding, painting, or attaching a handle. This kind of custom-made wagon is just as valuable as a store-bought one, and sometimes it is more appreciated.

Depending upon the interest of the teacher and available help from any skillful family members, various other transportation items can be constructed: a play boat, a rocket, a simple scooter. A teacher discovered a visiting retired carpenter (a granduncle of one of the children) who was delighted to practice his trade before the admiring group and to construct anything for and with them.

All activity, dramatic play, and talk about travel can naturally lead to, or can be deliberately guided to, a study and an awareness of transportation in nature. Appreciation of motion in nature entails scientific as well as philosophic and poetic observations. A young child becomes deeply aware of traveling birds by watching them, listening to stories about them, and looking at pictures of birds. Experience with mechanical human flight enables a child to appreciate the flight mechanism and motivates further interest in birds.

Butterflies are very attractive to children! When they chase the darting, flying creatures, they also notice how butterflies get around. Tiny beetles, inconspicuous compared to butterflies, provide curious small children with a stunning demonstration of wing power.

"How did he do it?" exclaimed three-year-old Jerry in astonishment when a stationary spotted ladybug he was watching on his arm suddenly revealed its hidden wings and took off!

The power and speed of four-footed animals in addition to horses interest transportation-minded children. Through the media of books, pictures, and television, they become acquainted with jaguars, mustangs, and other automobile namesakes. Considering and appreciating wild animals can be a basis for learning more about them and becoming interested in protecting them. Such learning should extend to sea life and the travels and motions of plain and fancy fishes and small and large creatures of the deep.

Movement and travel of less conspicious and generally less appreciated animals, when they can be observed, provide another area of learning. These include the footless swift, snake; the slow, two-footed chicken with its balanced tread; the sticky, one-footed snail; and the slug with its shapeless body. Each animal going his own distinctive way, fulfilling his purpose in life, causes children to ask, "How does he do it?" They are curious to know, and they patiently observe to find out and to compare a creature's locomotion with their own.

The world of related living, moving things consists not only of humans and other animals, but also of plants. Plants do not stand still. When a tree begins its life, it is *way down low* on the ground, but as it lives and grows, it goes up and up, higher and higher, slowly and surely reaching a height greater than any other living thing. A wild grapevine clings and climbs, going up and around and down a tree, making an intricately tangled course. A seed travels; it can drop to the ground and roll sometimes for a considerable distance. A tiny, tiny seed gets wafted into the air, riding the air currents, crossing the terrain, and surviving stormy weather. A seed can *live* through frost and long deep burial. Then, when favorable conditions of air, soil, and moisture occur, it starts a new life, growing out of its simple seed capsule into a complicated plant structure far away from its first home. So every living thing on earth swims, flies, runs, glides, or in one word *travels* in all seasons of the year.

Earth itself is a moving sphere, speedily turning in space. It is a safe traveler that has been whirling a million or so years without stopping!

9 Safety: Awareness in Action

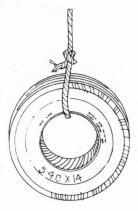

Teachers are probably aware of the responsibility that they have for the safety of other people's children in their charge. "As long as children are safe. . .," they are likely to say, implying that all else is of secondary importance. Parents' first concern about a preschool is rightly whether the facilities and program are safe for young children. Teachers know how impulsive, how lacking in judgment, how helpless and vulnerable little children are. Certainly, they want to protect the children from every possible physical harm.

But what does "safety for preschool children" mean in terms of responsibilities and early childhood learning? How is safety of the environment determined? Is a safety program good when children are merely physically intact? Should teachers be concerned only with instilling obedience to safety rules?

There is general agreement that the preschool years are an appropriate time to learn anything of a personal, concrete, human nature. It is also an appropriate time for learning communication skills and motor coordination, developing ability to avoid specific dangers, and reaching out to understand safe behavior. Another widely held conviction is that little children learn by several different methods: imitation, sensory exploration, firsthand experience, and wise encouragement. At the same time, learning can be seriously impaired by the fear and insecurity to which small children sometimes succumb.

A five-year-old boy had learned to use the self-service elevator in his apartment building and enjoyed using it alone. Then one day a policeman near the elevator door said to him, "Where are you going, kid?" The little boy felt intimidated and wanted to avoid repetition of the encounter for fear he would next be taken to jail. He refused to use the elevator alone for months afterward.

Since a preschool program is intended to provide a friendly, secure environment, such a program is ideal for learning about safety. Accurate, on-the-spot information about danger and safety is very important for young children. If this information comes from teachers who avoid anxiety themselves, the children become aware of danger without becoming anxious.

"Firemen do not make fires. Never," the teacher said during a discussion when a child conveyed or implied a notion to the contrary.

"The man seated high on the telephone pole is tied with a strong belt, and he has special hooks on his shoes to help him get down," she explained when children watching a telephone mechanic commented on his either falling or being unable to come down.

"Follow the signal and walk straight across the street. That's the best way!" stated the teacher clearly in preparation for street crossing.

"I'll help you make the bridge steady first, then you can walk across it safely," she told a child helpfully when he attempted to use an unstable structure.

The child can absorb and integrate such knowledge when it has this kind of immediate relevance to him. He also interprets the adult's communication as being in his behalf or for his good. As a result the child begins to feel secure about himself and his environment, and important conditions for learning safety are established.

Particular locations may have their own problems and safety requirements which are not present in other locations. However, the principles of positive approach in protecting children and in helping them learn practical lessons apply in any situation. It is therefore profitable to discuss some of the most common areas of safety.

Unquestionably traffic safety concerns most communities in the United States and is a vital part of a young child's life. Children's strong *interest* in transportation is a good basis for clear-cut, positive statements about many conditions within the scope of children's experiences, such as crossing streets and running toward a moving car in a driveway. The attitude is: it is good to go places in cars but not at all good to get hurt by them. In any conversation about danger in traffic, a child is likely to respond with: "You'll get killed." "You'll smash up." "Your head will get cut off." Such gory predictions spoken by a child almost casually or dramatically have an entirely different impact than when a grown-up, especially anyone in authority, makes similar drastic statements to children. Dire predictions from a grown-up cause some children to feel threatened with loss of life and limb or to become deeply fearful. Fear is not conducive to controlled safe behavior. It is important to elicit obedience from young children, but the reason for such obedience should be explained to them. Adults obey traffic regulations, but they understand that these regulations protect them.

Traffic safety regulations apply also to behavior in a vehicle: for example, rules pertaining to doors, safe ways of getting in and out, safe seating, and use of safety belts. If the rules are applied consistently and with confidence by adults, children can sense the protection and security, though sometimes they misinterpret such rules for punishment.

A teacher can learn much about children's knowledge, misconceptions, feelings, and fears by watching and listening to their dramatic play about safety.

In one way or another fire is a reality in every child's life, and it is strongly attractive to many if not most young children. Without reading grim statistics, teachers know from mass media reports, if not from their own experiences, about children causing fires and perishing in fires. It is, therefore, especially urgent for teachers in any kind of a preschool program to help children learn about fire safety.

Four-year-old Susan told her mother, "When I grow up, I want to do dangerous things."

On questioning Susan, the mother realized that Susan was not allowed to do such exciting things as lighting a match or turning on the gas jet because they were "dangerous."

A teacher can help children find out about the nature of fire.

Some people believe that the only effective way of teaching children is to deliberately let them get burned, and thus through pain they are conditioned not to go near a fire. This implies that children's curiosity is automatically squelched by fear of pain, and therefore fire ceases to be attractive. Certainly we cannot be sure of that! Is it not also possible that such treatment could result in a child's *resentment* toward an adult who administers pain in cold blood and in a child's panicky fear of fire? Experiencing pain from getting burned does not lead to understanding the nature of fire or to the need for controlled behavior.

A teacher should strive, therefore, to make fire understandable to children through classroom activities. Lighting candles for a child's birthday may occur as early as the first week of school. The teacher may attend to it in a perfunctory adult way: striking a match and putting it out, lighting candles and giving no thought to the act of causing match and candlewick to burn, and giving no word of explanation. However, it should be remembered that the process is fascinating to children, and the teacher should caution them about being too near, stating that lighting matches is a grown-up's task. She may let a child blow out the match. She might even light several matches if others ask for a chance to put out a match flame. Children in this situation are getting to know about fire under supervision.

Another common experience with fire comes when children and the teacher do any kind of cooking. Even in preparation of something as simple as instant cocoa, fire is involved in boiling the water. The teacher may be observing safety by expediently attending to boiling the water herself without saying anything. However, since she has the children's interest and attention, here is an opportunity to *show* why boiling water or steam is too hot to handle. She may cautiously put her finger near the pot or let a child hold his hand near the steam. The mere *sight* of steam does not tell children it is hot.

As a teacher was using an electric toaster with children, she became aware of the fact that several of them did not realize there was *an electric fire inside,* for they had never seen it. They had only watched the bread drop down and the toast pop up. Intelligent and safe behavior can be expected of children only if they have had some experience that includes a chance to ask questions and receive rational answers.

Although one seldom hears of a teacher actually making an

open fire for young children, I found it to be a significant learning experience, giving children knowledge and security.

It is late in the fall. The ground is dry, the trees are bare, a rough wind is blowing. The teacher herself has no enthusiasm for being outdoors, but the children scamper vigorously and find many things. Four-year-old Philip becomes excited when he finds two enormous sticks, which he drags along and wants to save for "guns." The sticks impede his movements and cause some trouble, so the teacher advises him to drop them.

"May I bring smaller sticks to school?" Philip wants to know, because he is specially interested in handling sticks. Other children, too, are interested in the variety and size and possible uses of sticks.

"Can you make a fire with sticks?" Philip asks eagerly and yet incredulously, as if he suddenly remembered hearing something about fire with sticks. "A real fire? . . . Could we make a fire in school?" The conversation about making a fire attracts all the children, and the possibility of their gathered sticks being used for that fire stimulates them to make further collections. When the children get back to class, one of them says seriously, "We can't make a fire in our room, though."

"Oh, no," the teacher answers equally seriously, and indicates a spot on the paved area in the yard where it might be possible to build a fire. She then suggests that bricks be gathered to make a safe fence for the fire.

"How do you make a *fire*?" a little girl asks, and her naive manner implies that she has *no* idea what goes into it. The teacher explains simply the elemental process.

"Can we do it *tomorrow* if we get the bricks?" they ask eagerly.

"If it's not windy," the teacher answers. The four-year-olds, always eager to explore and to learn — especially when confronted with as fascinating a phenomenon as fire — react not so much with disappointment about putting off their fire-making as with *wonder* about the role of the wind.

"Is today windy?" Philip with two others immediately run out to investigate. They are all excited, in spite of the teacher's calmness about the "dangers" of making a bonfire.

The preparation lasts several days. The sticks are saved in the closet and inspected daily, especially by Philip. The bricks are collected and played with and saved in the yard. The weather is analyzed for its windiness. One day it rains, so the children learn how that would prevent making a fire. Finally the day comes. The teacher shows them the matches she is going to use; and they gather outside around the pile of sticks, the circle of bricks, and the cans of water. The children, so independent and free in their usual activities and behavior in nursery school, are now careful to obey the teacher's instruction to sit on blocks at the prescribed distance from the bricks. In such a situation children accept readily the teacher's rules and controls.

The fourteen children are seated in a circle, each clutching some of the sticks and watching with wonder as the teacher strikes a match and makes a fire with small twigs and paper. The children then hand her more sticks, and soon a fire is flickering and flaming in front of the children. They are awed and quiet for a while; then one of them asks, "Can fire hurt you?" And the teacher reads some fear and caution in that question, with which several of the children are concerned, as she tells them again about the reason for bricks and for the distance of their seats. She tells them again about the use of water. Questions and comments keep coming as the children watch the fire.

"What will happen to the sticks from the fire?" The question shows the teacher that little children don't *know* about fire being able to consume an object like a stick.

"The stick will change," she answers, "you'll soon see." The children continue watching intently to see what the fire does.

"I see smoke!" one child exclaims. Another one blinks and says with surprise, "The smoke goes in my eyes!" and the children shift their seats to avoid the windblown smoke. The teacher puts on the rest of the children's sticks and a small log, which burn brightly and invitingly and add to the relaxation and pleasure.

"Look, the fire is bigger!" someone observes.

"I *smell* the fire!" adds another, and they all wrinkle their noses and sniff to verify this observation. Philip puts his hand out tentatively.

"It feels hot on my hand," he says. Then the children take turns holding a hand close to the fire, and feeling the good warmth on a cold day. Now the flames are dying down, and the children regret it. But the teacher says it is time to put the fire out, and tells them they may pour the water on it—another new sensation to add to learning, another impression as the children pour cans of water.

"I hear it sizzle."

"It smells different now." They watch intently as the last whiff of smoke and steam disappear. They touch the bits of charcoal and feel the remaining warmth on the bricks.

The bricks become important, for the children continue playing with them for several days afterward, arranging them for a fireplace and pretending to be making a fire, with appropriate crackling and sizzling sounds and gestures of feeling warmth. "Playing with fire" together, the children seem to reinforce their impressions, to articulate the personal meaning of the group experience in making a real fire.*

*From *Living and Learning in Nursery School* by Marguerita Rudolph. New York: Harper & Row, Publishers, 1954, pp. 43–46.

Since there are official fire regulations in every community, preschool children must become acquainted with them in an appropriate way. A *fire drill* is such a regulation. Before a fire drill is held, it is necessary to talk with children. What does *fire drill* mean? Most children, not knowing the word *drill*, say it is *fire*. The teacher needs to define it as practice in getting out of the building safely, to explain that there will be no fire when there is a fire drill, to indicate the exit door for leaving the building safely and quickly, and to demonstrate how to obey the signal. She might say something like: "I am sure you can do it and I will help you." Then she gives children a chance to ask questions or to express worries. A child may want to know how the bell is rung. One or more children may already be afraid of fire, or may now become afraid. The teacher must reassure those children personally, and still remain confident and practical about conducting a fire drill. In general, the whole dramatic procedure involving response to bell, stopping all activity at once, lining up (which may be a novelty to preschoolers), and proceeding to a designated spot is really fun. The fact that other children do it willingly and successfully usually convinces the fearful ones that they need have no anxiety.

The subject of fire drills sometimes is followed naturally by a group discussion on detecting fire by smelling or hearing and also discussion about checking on possible sources of fire when leaving the house. Children want to know how they can have a hand in putting fires out, even on a small scale. A teacher may suggest such precautionary measures as snuffing out burning candles, smothering a small fire with handfuls of dirt or sand, and dousing smoldering coals with water.

A visit to a firehouse in the neighborhood is an exciting trip, mainly because of the shiny fire trucks, the dramatic gear of firemen, and an opportunity perhaps to ring the bell on the truck. Unfortunately, the fireman guide is often either sentimental and condescending (or worse) in his attitude. He may insist on giving them a technical lecture. One fireman, after a lengthy lecture, told a class of fidgety four- and five-year-olds sternly, "If your house catches on fire, don't you hide under the bed — or you'll burn up." Several children heard only the last phrase and believed that they actually would burn up that very night. However, a relaxed, informal visit to the firehouse facilities with inspection of fire-fighting equipment and sensible casual acquaintance with firemen contributes to children's basic knowledge and feeling of security. What impressed one group of children most on their visit was the fireman's demonstration (which he repeated at their request) of how quickly he climbed a high ladder and how tough his helmet and boots were. He let the children put on his boots. After that encounter the children had faith in firemen.

Another significant area of learning safety in the preschool years is in use of large equipment by many children during free outdoor play. Ample stationary jungle gyms, ladders of all kinds, slides for swift descent, seesaws, platforms or boxes for jumping off, and boards for bouncing and balancing are such standard equipment. They constitute a familiar sight and are indeed used vigorously by all healthy children. Young growing boys and girls require enjoyable physical activity and adventure. They try to climb to the highest rung of the jungle gym or into the tree on a rope ladder, or turn upside down and hang by the heels, or stand on something higher than themselves as they gather courage and jump down. These physical explorations are exhilarating to the spirit and satisfying in terms of achievement and self-importance. The value of such activity is clearly present, but so is a certain amount of danger. A child might slip, stumble, lose his balance or grip and thus get hurt. Supervision during outdoor play is, therefore, a commonsense must. Even then, not all accidents can be prevented, however protective and watchful teachers are.

Bruises, scratches, splinters, falls, and bumps create distress for children and adults. Though immediate first-aid measures are required to fix the harm, solutions that will help prevent the repetition of accidents are needed. Avoiding repetition of an accident and learning from a bad experience constitute educational tasks for children and teachers. If children wearing short pants get scrapes on their knees from the pavement, they may be advised to change to longer pants. If someone gets a splinter in his hand from a sandbox seat, the teacher not only removes the splinter and fixes the child's hand, but also makes the wood on the seat safely smooth. A stumble and fall over a block lying in the running area can result in a safety rule agreed to by all children: Keep the riding and running yard space clear.

One logical way of accident prevention is to routinely inspect all outdoor equipment. Boys as well as girls delight in detecting danger, such as a loose or splintery board, a nail out of place, or a fallen branch. The delight is still greater if they take part in hammering or pulling a nail and fixing their own equipment. Even by watching a grown-up fix something, with a chance to talk about the work and hold a tool, children gain respect for repairs as related to their safety.

In one school a conscientious check was kept of all accidents. The form which the teacher filled out contained only basic information: child's name, date, time, what happened, home contact, treatment, consequence. After three months the chart revealed that the greatest number of accidents occurred toward the end of a day's session. The staff's commonsense conclusion was that accidents are likely to happen when children and teachers are more tired and lax. For the sake of safety it was, therefore, advisable to initiate quiet, relaxing activities before going home, and the teachers recognized the need to be especially alert about safety at that time.

People seeing for the first time such small children using the large equipment are aghast at the sight, probably visualizing a catastrophic plunge or twist by one of those daredevils. Some parents are alarmed at the presence of equipment and possible consequences of young children's boldness. Other parents, seeing other children in action, begin urging their own more hesitant, cautious children to "go on! See how that little girl does it? Isn't she great?" However, children do not like to be pushed or shamed into action; if they are, often they react with confusion, resistance, and loss of whatever interest they had.

The purposes of having such inviting equipment are, of course, for children to exercise their growing muscles, to have an outlet for their abundant physical energies, to develop body strength and coordination of large muscles and courage. Each child confronts and conquers a steep slide or a vertical or horizontal climb in his own style and at his own pace. He assesses himself, his readiness and ability. Some children may want an adult to stand by for a while; some are fearful and want only to watch. Some may be hesitant and some simply prudently cautious. Some children are bold at the start then decide to take it easy. In which case it is no use for an adult to complain and say, "You did it yesterday, so why can't you do it today? Go on!" A child has to develop confidence in his own way in order to engage in controlled safe activity and develop further skill in using a particular piece of equipment.

The teacher must make sure that the safety rules for each piece of equipment are understood by children: *Feet first* down a slide for safe landing. *No more than two* (or three) children on the playhouse roof so no one will get pushed. When rolling a heavy tire, look and *get people out of the way* first. My impression is that children in preschools have far fewer accidents than children of the same age in homes, due mainly to the preschools' supervision and safety of good equipment.

There is one piece of popular standard playground equipment which I find least desirable from the point of view of both safety and good exercise for young children. This is the stationary swing — often a whole row of swings. Children are likely to run impulsively and they are usually unable to judge the distance of an object in motion. They cannot understand the possibility of getting knocked down by a moving swing until it actually happens to them. This puts the teacher in a position of having to make nagging reminders and of being always on the "nervous lookout." A possible solution would be to close off the area around the swing, or replace a seat swing with one tire swing which can be operated by several children and provide friendly, rather than solitary activity. A tire swing offers much more physical challenge and exercise than a conventional swing and presents less danger of another child's being knocked down. The tire suspended by rope from a stout limb of a tree on the playground enables the child to enjoy a self-propelled, rhythmic motion and feel in contact with a living creation of nature!

There are areas requiring safety consideration indoors as well. Stairs constitute one such area. Small children need to be advised to use banisters and to avoid crowding. Doors can also be hazardous and need to be especially watched since preschool children are often tempted to play "opening and shutting" without regard for catching their own or someone else's hands in either side of a door. Children seem incapable of understanding this potential danger. Sometimes the situation warrants removal of an interior door or perhaps installation of a sliding door made of soft material.

Learning about safety enables other kinds of learning to take place. Children become better observers, keener detectives, more active, intelligent helpers, and they feel secure about safety in their environment. Teachers learn to think ahead, to watch with many eyes, to understand children, and to be aware of children's lack of knowledge and understanding. In practicing different kinds of protection, teachers become even more caring about children.

10 The Child as a Multimedia Artist

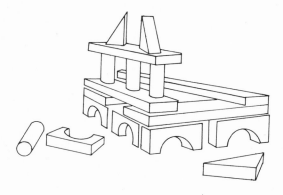

The aim of this chapter is to look at the young child's artistic interests in handling various available materials and trying various forms of expression in music, in movement, and in performing.

Although some children may quite early indicate special response to music, or be able to make impressive designs on paper, or show recognizable artistic talent with other media, *all* children respond to some kind of art media. The young child is basically a multimedia artist.

Given a hunk of clay, the child may explore it by poking, pinching, pounding. He may produce flat, spherical, cylindrical, or built-on shapes, enjoying the tactile stimulation and the surprise visual results. In the process he may also become affected by the sound and rhythm of his work with clay: pat-pat-pat with the flat of the hand and whack with the fist. His nearby fellow artists catch the pattern and join in. Soon the activity may change: first, pound with the hard, tensed fist; then, roll and roll with an open hand; next, roll with both hands all the way across and even *off* the table. This is expressive body movement. Vocalization may occur as an accompaniment to the hand-clay rhythm, or may be a different simultaneous expression. So a piece of earthy, malleable clay affords a child tactile contact and rhythmic stimulation and the chance to create changeable shapes and make vocal and verbal responses.

Here is an account of an entirely different material that engaged the children's attention. A block building was in progress on a large section of the classroom floor. Three children were involved in the activity. The teacher watched to see what was happening: first an enclosure was extended, next a wall rose, and then an exit was planned. At that moment a fourth child appeared on the scene clutching a new boat and, thus, attracted the attention of the builders.

"Let's see your boat! Put it here, right here!" beckoned one child.

"No! The boat can only go in water. Don't you know?" the owner replied.

Of course, the builders knew that, and since they felt so in harmony with the boatman, they were willing to "make a river," "no, a lake," for the boat. The sight of the boat stirred the imagination and propelled the builders into a different creative activity. Using crayons, they quickly drew big blue swishes and swatches on a large piece of paper and, obtaining the teacher's help, secured the paper to the floor with tape and surrounded it with a low block structure. They had unmistakably created water!

The originally skeptical boatman fell in with the builders' scheme, allowing his boat to be launched. A visitor, entering the room at that time, was told earnestly, "Watch out! Don't step in the water." All within the context of spontaneous play and of creative use of materials and social relationships, the children simply changed from building a structure to producing scenic design to dramatic pretending.

Sometimes a child shows a distinct preference for a particular medium, but he usually does not stay away from other media for long. He may find special satisfaction in the blocks, may know what to expect from their rigidity and their definite dimensions, and may enjoy using his strength in handling and hauling the sturdy blocks. This child may only take a quick look at the painting area in the class and pass it by. Pasting and cutting and other small muscle manipulation may occasionally hold his attention briefly, after which he is glad to return to block building and to a sure success. Then one day just as the teachers are wondering if this child will ever paint or at least try this popular activity, they observe him stopping by the easel, contemplating the blank space on paper and the row of clear poster colors with brushes. Then with spontaneous strokes and full attention he creates a unique, complete composition that *pleases him!* "I want to take it home," he says. After that he may paint frequently. Perhaps he realizes the advantage that a painting has over a block building — that is, he can take the painting home. Or, perhaps he is now ready for a change. The teacher may not know why, but she knows it happens. Children's interests do change.

Jenny was a familiar figure by the easels, making varied strokes, pushing up drips from the brushes, and producing different color effects and a variety of pleasing surprising patterns. Teachers and children alike admired Jenny's paintings. Then one day gentle Jenny made a small block building at the very edge of the building area. However, as soon as she saw several boys rushing up to the shelf and hauling piles of blocks onto the floor, Jenny without saying anything abandoned her building and ran toward the easels.

Another girl, braver with words, said, "The boys don't let us make buildings."

The teacher overheard this and was appalled that she herself had not even noticed such sex discrimination. She had been taking for granted the boys' enjoyment of building, as though they were specially entitled to it. Having learned a lesson from the children, the teacher promptly saw to it that everyone who wanted to build and might have been discouraged by the particularly aggressive boys had time and space for building and freedom from intrusion. Not only justice was done, but also a unique, beautiful block building soon came into view, including delicate decorative and functional structures by Jenny.

One winter a teacher who took weekly stock of predominant group activities noticed that there had been considerable decrease in the children's art work with the standard materials. After asking herself *what* the children were doing recently that required creative energy, it became clear to the teacher that they were indeed enjoying a uniquely pleasurable and to them an artistic perishable medium, the abundant snow in the play yard. They loved handling, investigating, and playing with it, even bringing a bowlful of white snow inside and sprinkling it with paint colors! The teacher concluded that the children were having a creative fling with snow while it lasted and were using the opportunity to rest up from indoor materials.

Since a child is a multimedia artist and is a whole, integrated, growing, changing human being, it seems arbitrary to regard art in terms of a particular medium. The teacher needs to *focus* on separate media or groups of media to understand the challenges, to assess the practical problems, and to take a fresh look at children under a special stimulation.

What strikes an adult first in seeing creative expression in children is their free use of the body. A preschool program must allow for expression and cultivation of movement and music, including exploration of sound. Children like to practice, to see and hear artistic performance, and to *perform* with and for others in the general areas of music, dance, and drama. Children even younger than three years of age have considerable imagination and are capable of make-believe play, of using pantomime, and even of clowning. They can be involved in dressing up without any self-consciousness.

In a medium as different as the performing arts, teachers should keep in mind, of course, that the goal of a preschool is not the training of performers, but the providing of various aids to creative expression. A program should also provide some exposure to the performing arts that are appropriate to the children's age and would encourage them to try out different forms and styles of performance. Depending upon their interests, children may enjoy different kinds of recordings: folk songs, dance music, instrumental music, and poetry reading.

In a preschool center during World War II, four-year-old Freddie, an Austrian refugee who had hardly any knowledge of the English language, was involved in dramatic play.[1] He was truly playing the role of a rabbi. He summoned the children, beckoned to them with appropriate gestures, and draped an old cloth around himself with such impressive dignity that others knew for sure the cloth was a prayer shawl. His facial expression, his swaying and bowing body, and his hands were all involved. Freddie began with soft mumbling from a "prayer book," his voice rising in rhythmic chant and changing to an assertive singsong as he used real Hebrew words. There was a prescribed end to the prayer, and Freddie changed both his performance and facial expression accordingly. Looking jovial then, he shook hands, repeating the salutation: "Goot Shabbos."

[1] Marguerita Rudolph. "This Is Freddie." In *Common Ground* Magazine, winter issue, 1941, p. 45.

While enjoying Freddie's performance, the teachers learned what they needed to do to promote continuation and satisfaction. They obtained old sheeting and cut a few rectangular pieces that would be manageable to use as prayer shawls. They also borrowed from parents a real prayer book to keep in the box with the prayer shawls. After a discussion with the children as to what was needed to play "synagogue," the teachers helped with construction of a sacred scroll. Since so many of the children (especially the boys) did attend the synagogue with parents or grandparents, they played the religious rituals with knowledge as well as with imagination.

Another of Freddie's experiences in the preschool center relates to his musical activity. The teacher informed the children about the school holiday honoring Abraham Lincoln's birthday. The knowing look that Freddie gave her made the teacher realize that he had heard about Lincoln, probably from an older sister. Later in the day when she called the children to the piano for singing, and asked if any one had a song in mind, Freddie came forth with: "Zing 'Happy Birthday' to Lincoln!"

"That's a good idea, Freddie," the teacher agreed.

So Freddie sang loud and clear all the English words, ending with "Happy birthday, dear Lincoln, Happy birthday to you."

Immediately after that success Freddie had a related idea for performance.

"Me!" knocking himself on the chest and announcing commandingly, "I—Lincoln. Lincoln—soldier."

He rose from his sitting position and made marching motions with arms and feet. The teacher picked up the rhythm on the piano and the children joined in for a vigorous march around the room. Another child had an idea for still a different dimension in performance, using instruments. So the teacher went into the closet and took out the box with simple rhythm instruments for the child. Everyone chose an instrument and engaged in a louder, stronger march. While the teacher watched the children marching, she realized that her repertory of marches was very limited. She decided she would learn other selections from fellow teachers and from different music sources.

Since marching soldiers constituted reality in Freddie's recent life, it was natural that he should attribute it to Lincoln, too. The teacher borrowed from the library a picture book about Lincoln, showing him in other occupations that were equally significant in his life. How Freddie studied those pictures!

Through participation in the arts children and teachers engage in considerable study to supplement knowledge, to investigate props, and to get ideas for construction and sometimes inspiration for creation. Freddie's teacher searched for books, pictures, period music, and records, all of which she shared with the children whose interest had been stimulated by Freddie.

Puppets, an attractive and distinctly theatrical art form, are more sophisticated for very young literal-minded preschool children than grown-ups assume. Although *watching* a puppet show is very enjoyable, it may be difficult for a child to assume the role of a puppet that is separate from him. However, many older preschool children can construct puppet stages, invent dialogue, and experience personal theatrical success. Sometimes flannelboard figures, so much more manageable than puppets, can serve a similar purpose.

A teacher has a great deal to do with supplies, supervision, and extra preparation to support the performing arts for and by the children. The quality and the significance of these responsibilities do not necessarily depend upon a generous budget or the performing skills of the teacher, although both are desirable and useful. Good rhythm instruments for children, record players (and their repairs), and good instruments for the teacher's use are expensive. A teacher who is skillful with an instrument or two or who has a musical voice seems to work magic with getting children's attention, often being attuned to their musical sensitivity or potential. Money alone cannot supply a musically congenial setting and cannot create an atmosphere conducive to freedom and creativity. Also, mere skills do not guarantee a giving spirit or discriminating taste or, what is most important, responsiveness to *children's ideas and originality.*

Among the teacher's concerns in providing for the performing arts is finding out what children are exposed to at home through ethnic culture and tradition and mass media. Such knowledge guides her in offering familiar and different music, balancing it with the traditional, modern and classical. In her exploration of musical home experiences, the teacher may learn that there is a young or an older musician or dancer who could come to perform for and with the children.

Eddie's grandfather was an amateur magician and was delighted to perform informally for Eddie's nursery group. He did simple, impressive acts, explained some of the tricks, and let the children try to do some. The closeness to the performer in their midst as well as his kindness and personal attention to them made each child watch everything with complete absorption and joy and excitement.

"The best audience I could have!" said the grandfather.

In the promotion of the arts the teacher needs to take stock of supplies quite regularly. Worn recordings may need to be discarded and those inappropriate for the time should be stored for later use. Some rhythm instruments may need simple repair, such as polishing the metal triangles if they are rusty and providing new handles for them and mending punctured drum heads. A child's parent or older brother could assist with these repairs. Small items such as a bell, bell bracelets, rhythm sticks, or shakers could be added to the collection of instruments. The box in which they are kept, hooks where they are hung, or the special shelf should be kept in a satisfactory condition so that respectful handling and storing of the instruments by children are encouraged. The teacher may decide with the children how to improve the keeping and care of instruments.

Props need to be acquired which facilitate or direct movement and dancing. These may be delicate colored scarfs, bright flowing ribbons, hoops to define an area or to move with, a sombrero, feathers, head bands, or still other props that can be bought inexpensively, borrowed, or made by the teachers, parents, or friends.

Making items for a performance is a natural creative project! The workmanship by children (and teachers) may be poor; the products may be far from perfect, and they may not last. Yet, the creative undertaking is full of interesting exploration and artistic surprises. Besides, anything made with one's own hands has an element of personal expression; it carries the individuality of the maker.

Following are "musical" items which are easily obtainable or assembled:

Drums — large enough, empty cylindrical cans and boxes with secure lids or heads and decorative covering.

Drum sticks — wooden spoons or old wooden handles with secure cloth heads.

Tambourines — double or triple paper plates (clean used ones are acceptable) with holes punched all around and strung with clattery bottle tops as well as with colorful ribbons or yarns.

Shakers—juice or other small aluminum cans that have been emptied through punctured holes, filled with pebbles or dry peas, then sealed, and perhaps decorated with glued-on cloth. *Sand blocks*—rectangular, hand-size pieces of wood, each with rough sandpaper glued to one side for rubbing together as pairs. *Guitar or banjo*—open, sturdy, rigid cigar boxes (or similar containers) with a few rubber bands of different thicknesses stretched parallel and lengthwise across them. Rubber bands stretched to different tightnesses can produce a musical scale. *Cymbals*—aluminum pots (or lids) and spoons.

Many other objects can be devised, constructed, invented, tailor-made for a rhythm band or for individual playing. When such an instrument collapses from vigorous use, children can have the pleasure of making another one, perhaps a better one.

In the *visual* arts of painting, drawing, collage construction, and creating with other materials, the child is an explorer, an experimenter, and an unpredictable stylist. An adult intending to make suggestions to the child artist might as well save his breath. Somebody else's idea or advice means very little if anything to the young child and may inhibit his work altogether. The same holds true for an adult presuming to know the subject of a young child's creation. Naming a picture may have nothing to do with either the process or the result. When a child, especially a younger one, is asked what he made, he is likely to become confused or think he *ought* to know what the picture represents, in which case he may invent a subject that might have no relation to his creation.

"Tell me about your picture," the teacher said solicitously as she was writing Mark's name on the painting.

"It's a big bear," he told her, elaborating on the size and making up a story to please the teacher.

In many instances an adult may see in a child's picture a subject or a representation that is not what the child intended.

"Are you finished?" the teacher asked Karl who stood before an easel and looked passively at his picture with blobs of different colors close to each other and one separate roundish form. "Is that an apple you painted?"

"No, that's the red light, don't you see? I am waiting for it to turn green, so I can get out of the traffic jam."

Karl had his own ideas about shapes, colors, use of space and representation of motion, and pace at which he worked.

This child was drawing flowers; around them she drew several dozen dots:

"What are those? Flies?"

"No. They are the fragrance of the flowers."*

If a teacher listens unobtrusively, she can hear children speak about their art work once in a while.

"I am going to make the blackest black."

"Now I make green inside."

"Now I make a line in the middle."

"Look! Drip, drip, drip."

Some teachers unfortunately prefer not to hear what the children are saying and follow instead their own notions of what art work should be.

Debby is seated at a table with three other children in a beautifully equipped and orderly kindergarten room. She has her own box of crayons and nice rough drawing paper.

Blue-eyed, long-haired Debby is working away with concentration, forming the image of a little girl with long hair. She adds details, fills in spaces, and emphasizes each space with a particular color she selects from a large assortment. The dominating color in Debby's picture is blue. Blue is the color in the flowery dress, blue in the spots of eyes, and blue is even the color of the hair!

"That's lovely, dear, but tell me: what color hair do people have?" Debby looks puzzled, almost startled, as if she were unprepared either to think or speak about it. She gives no answer. "What color is *your* hair?"

"Brown," Debby answers quietly and knowledgeably, but indicating in no way that she sees any relation between real hair color and the meaning or feeling in the blue hair of her drawing. The teacher now stops near another child and looks at the drawing of a person with rather straggly weak limbs. "Tell me, honey, where do the arms belong? Show me on you! That's *right*. On your shoulder, of course." Still another child shows the teacher a picture with people in it. After praising it the teacher asks cheerfully and humorously, "My goodness — did all their hair fall out?"

"No," the child answers, chagrined, and runs back to the drawing table to put hair on.†

*From *From Two to Five* by Kornei Chukovsky. Berkeley, Calif.: University of California Press, 1963.

†From: *Kindergarten: A Year of Learning* by Marguerita Rudolph and Dorothy H. Cohen. Copyright © 1964 by Meredith Publishing Company. By permission of Appleton-Century-Crofts, Educational Division, Meredith Corporation, p. 215.

In this account it is easy to recognize the inappropriateness of adult standards and realism with respect to anatomical correctness applied to children's art work. Such intrusion upon a child's imagination and feeling interferes with what he is trying to express and snuffs out the fun he has with his own artistic activity.

Some conscientious teachers presume to know what children *should* create for psychological reasons, as in the following incident.

The room was specially set up for an art session for about six children to work with paints. There were plenty of space and light, good materials, and an interested teacher, and the children were absorbed in what they were doing.

The teacher looked at five-year-old Randy's arrangement of strong, colorful shapes on the paper and said: "Let's talk about it."

Reticent at first, Randy told her haltingly about the water and the fishing scene he had painted.

"See?" Randy pointed to what appeared to be a big fishing line.

"And what's this little thing?" the teacher wanted to know.

"That's me fishing—here's the line," the child artist stated.

"Oh, you'll have to make yourself bigger than that," the teacher stated authoritatively, and added a psychological lesson. "You are the most important part, so you should make yourself bigger. *Right?*"

Randy's face looked indifferent, but his head nodded.

"Make some flesh color now," she told Randy.

He did. He obliged the teacher—but at what cost to his artistic and personal integrity!

While criticism can adversely affect a child and his work, excessive praise can, too.

When Helen painted spontaneously a pattern of parallel light-colored waves, the teacher exclaimed joyfully, "Oh, that's beautiful!" before Helen had a chance to appreciate what she had made.

"Look, Miss Andrews, what Helen painted!" the teacher called enthusiastically to her assistant.

Although Helen may not have finished her work, she stopped, looking thrilled with the sudden special recognition. Other fellow artists nearby were jolted by the teacher's unfamiliar outburst of praise. They looked enviously and carefully at the *cause célèbre* and then they *also* painted horizontally inclined waves. And Helen's next and *next* paintings? Yes—parallel waves. The teachers finally understood their role in creating this situation and learned from their mistake.

It is difficult to be a good teacher in many instances. It is difficult to refrain from praising and at other times difficult to give praise, especially when requested by a child.

"Look at this, Miss Morris!" a child called, pointing to his painting as though sharing his satisfaction with the teacher.

"I *like* it," she answered warmly and without elaboration.

The child was happy with such acceptance of his creation (and therefore, of himself). Acceptance was all he wanted. The teacher did not feel she was required to give any "artistic" judgment or interpretation. But sometimes children want an opinion.

"Do you think this picture is nice?" Mary asked, looking the teacher straight in the eye.

"Of course it's nice!" the teacher answered with deliberate approval, as though it would be unthinkable to say "it's not nice."

But Mary did not appear convinced.

"I don't think it's nice. I hate it," she stated rather calmly.

Was Mary challenging the teacher's sincerity? Was she asking for proof that her picture was nice? Then Mary indicated that she was going to tear up the picture.

"You worked so hard at it, Mary!" the teacher said quickly. "And it didn't come out badly. I think it's worth saving."

Mary's changed expression then showed she was reconsidering. The teacher qualified her defense of Mary's picture further.

"You used beautiful colors," she said. "How did you make that delicate pink?"

Mary's expression began to change as she, too, admired the pink.

"I mixed it with red and white!" she explained proudly now.

She decided to save her picture, and she put it in her take-home bag. Apparently the *specifics* of "hard work" and "beautiful colors" and that special "pink" which the teacher had not overlooked had a ring of truth to Mary's ears.

The sensible advice then when faced with having to give praise or criticism is to be concrete and constructive. Sometimes a noncommittal "let me look at it some more" helps until the teacher finds an honest response. Comment should be *about the work* and not about the child.

In being a multimedia artist, a child is a multisensory artist, especially with the variety of materials that are now available, such as thick, dusty chalk pastels, various Magic Markers of intense hues, and smeary finger paints (bought or made). The materials chosen by the teacher should be those that serve the children well, whether they enrich their visual experience, stimulate imagination, or afford artistic discoveries *and* are manageable by children without requiring undue supervision and too much housekeeping.

A teacher has to remind herself that the art *medium itself* can be of major importance to the child. Certainly the *newness* of an art material demands that the child have time, first, to feel and to understand the material (to have contact with it), next, to experience the process of using it, and, then, to be concerned with the result. Colored chalk, for instance, is fun to rub, just rub and rub until only a powdery mass is left. Or, spoonfuls of finger paint are quickly absorbed into hands, and more and more of it is demanded by children to enjoy (or wallow in)—"hand-immersion" and "paint-dispersion" rather than actual finger painting. While affording children the opportunity to explore a medium, the teacher must also be practical. It is too expensive and wasteful to use up materials immediately. The teacher, therefore, needs to consider the purpose for which the materials are used, and limit use of them or curtail the activity accordingly. For example, when a box of new, bright-colored pipe cleaners is opened, some children may want very much to take a big bunch *just to hold them* because it feels good to have an ample quantity of something appealing and tactile. After children (who want to) hold and feel the pipe cleaners, these items can be put back in the box. The teacher may also realistically *ration* the pipe cleaners for construction. Poster paint may be pleasant to pour, but not to pour *out* on paper! Tape is interesting to stick on and stick on, but it needs to be *used* to attach things. With experience, even young children understand. However, if controlled use of a particular material causes only frustration to the children, perhaps the teacher should consider delaying the use of it for awhile and offer instead a medium with which they can be freer and which can be reused, such as play dough or clay.

It is also important for a teacher to recognize which art material may be difficult for her to manage. For instance, she may be quite responsive to the fullness of pleasure that finger painting provides for children, but at the same time she is aware that the activity also makes her work half an hour extra, that she groans while scrubbing sides of tables and sinks where the children washed their hands. A teacher should, but often is unable to, devise a satisfactory self-help arrangement for finger painting. In that case perhaps she should consider *other* materials that are fluid, and tactile, and responsive to manipulation—materials which can be used freely and pleasurably by children and which do not impose extra cleaning chores. Among such materials are easel paints (used with protective smocks), water with some color in it, and gooey mud (used outdoors weather permitting).

Selection of materials also then becomes a special challenge in the art of collage. Everything and anything may be right for collage. So the challenge for teachers and children is discrimination and *selectivity* and manageable *variety* of natural as well as commercial materials. Keeping collage materials in orderly usable condition may also be a problem. Yet the process as well as the result is interesting and stimulating and provides much fun for all ages. In addition, collage materials cost practically nothing (discounting paste or glue and even that can be inexpensively made).

Although ordinary manila drawing paper may be firm enough to be used as a base to attach paper shapes and light materials, cardboard is definitely preferable. Readily available sources include shirt board from commercially laundered shirts (which some families may have on hand) and cardboard from different kinds of packaging. Adequate sized pieces of cardboard can be cut from discarded boxes. Each child needs to have his own small container (or no more than two children share one) for holding the paste. Such a container can be devised from used paper cups cut to size, discarded metal jar lids, or folded rimmed pieces of used aluminum. Equipped with cardboard and the holder with paste, the child next surveys the big box or basket with "stuff" and *then* begins the process of *selecting* separate pieces of shapes, colors, textures, and dimensions: pieces of interesting paper or cloth or synthetics, bright and shiny and smooth; curls of wood shavings; dark specks of grain; flat fruit seeds; pieces of colored drinking straws; etc. The child arranges and secures his selection of materials to the cardboard base as he completes his artistic experience.

Too much "stuff" can be overwhelming and confusing and also too exciting. Thus, controlling the *quantity* of materials is a constant challenge to the teacher. Yet, enough variety of materials is necessary for artistic use, and children love *abundance* itself. Generally, one box with about five compartments of different materials in each serves four or five children quite well.

However, a teacher can best determine for herself the most work-able distribution of materials and children.

Wood for woodworking activity is another popular nursery school and kindergarten material that commands multisensory responses from children and is often an art medium. All pre-schoolers, girls as well as boys, show interest in using wood; they enjoy touching, handling, and keeping pieces of wood. They explore spontaneously the various properties, including the smell of different woods. They like especially the use of *real* tools that go with woodworking. The process of sawing and severing wood, of hammering nails *into* it, and of attaching objects to it engages them thoroughly. This process calls for coordination and concentration and provides experience in basic mechanics. Yet the *overall* pleasurable activity of using wood and making some-thing tangible and surprising that a child can hold and keep is creative.

Amy sanded a thick rectangular piece of pine wood and per-sisted in hammering nails into it until she hammered "a whole bunch." The nails kept bending under her strikes, but she pulled each bent one out with the claw of the hammer and added a new one. At last she produced two rows of firmly driven yet upright nails. After admiring the result she picked out a couple of colored rubber bands and stretched them across the nails. Her expression revealed that Amy had a treasure to take home!

Of all the different art media and the so-called "learning mate-rials," as well as of all the play equipment used in classrooms for children from three to six years of age, the standard unit building blocks offer most in multiple values to children. Unfortunately, in many classrooms throughout the country, blocks are often over-looked and disregarded by teachers and supervisors. In such class-rooms blocks are either not presented to children at all or they are misused or ignored by children.

Following is a graphic account of the role of blocks in early childhood curriculum by the late, well-known creative educator Lucy Sprague Mitchell.

Toy makers have put blocks on the market for many long years, decorating them with letters of the alphabet in an attempt to sneak some-thing "useful" into a child's play. But small children usually ignored the letters and piled the blocks into gay towers. Then, some thirty or more years ago, school people began to take children's play seriously, to say that play itself was educational, and a different kind of blocks came on the market. They were just pieces of unpainted wood, the same width and thickness, and with lengths twice or four times as great as the unit block. A few curves, cylinders, and half-thickness blocks were added, but all with lengths that fitted into the measurements of the basic blocks.

Many schools for young children now use these blocks. They have been found to be the most useful tool for self-education that young children can play with and work with.

These blocks in the creative hands of children also become an art medium. Grown-ups are still prone to organize a curriculum for one "area of learning" and then for another, and to work out equipment which they think will develop one patch of a child and then another. But children just refuse to respond in this piecemeal fashion. They remain consistently whole people, reacting to situations with all their lively interests mixed together. They are small scientists eagerly investigating the world that they can lay their hands on; small human beings interested in other human beings; dramatists playing out their experiences, modifying them to give themselves a strategic position in the world of grown-ups; workmen exulting in their techniques; artists enjoying design and pattern-form, balance in size and color, repetition. The wonder of blocks is the many-sided constructive experiences they yield to the many-sided constructive child — and every child is such if guided by a many-sided constructive parent or teacher.*

Block building is considered important for young children because it requires so much broad physical involvement: getting down on the floor; carrying and placing solid objects; handling and balancing; erecting, extending, and removing — all are physical, naturally performed operations. As children become absorbed in block building, they explore floor space, the dimensions of blocks, the relation of fitness of different shapes. Thus, children put whatever knowledge they have gained promptly to use. This is shown beautifully in a block-building film[2] where children strive for delicate balance as well as for stability and achieve satisfaction with the visible, tangible results of block building. Visible is the satisfaction of an artist in the child's facial and bodily expression that says: "I made it!" May not this satisfaction and even pride become part of him as a growing person, as an artist-learner?

*From The Art of Block Building by Harriet M. Johnson; in the "Introduction" by Lucy Sprague Mitchell. New York: Bank Street College Publications.

[2] Blocks, A Medium of Perceptual Learnings. Produced in cooperation with Queens College (Mary Moffitt, consultant). Campus Film Productions, Inc., New York.

A child experiences artistic satisfaction also from objects made specially for him by adults. Katie adored her tin-can pail, made by her father at a parents' evening workshop in her class. It was painted red, and red became her favorite color. It had a string handle, so the technique of attaching handles fascinated Katie. Her name on the pail (distinguishable to her) was a pleasure for her to behold. Timmy on the other hand treasured a miniature hand-size pillow which was made for him by a relative. He knew that it was stuffed with feathers. He pointed to the sewed ticking material and called attention to the pillowcase with a border exactly like the "real one" on which he slept.

There is no clear-cut distinction for young children between art and craft objects, materials, and activities. This applies especially to the many common and timeless household materials that can be enjoyed in a preschool program. These materials are innumerable, though only a few are considered here to suggest variety and uses and to encourage the teacher to search for others.

Collection of buttons Buttons can probably be obtained from grandmothers, rather than from mothers who may tend to use mostly zippers. Inexpensive buttons may be purchased to supplement the collection. New ones are attractive, but they are second best compared to old ones from particular garments: men's suits and jackets, ladies' coats, children's shirts, baby rompers, etc.

A large assortment kept in a special button box stimulates interest and use. A *few* children at a time can explore and play with buttons: sorting and arranging and enjoying the *different* colors, textures (wood, metal, cloth, glass, etc.), shapes, and construction (holes in different places). Individual children may borrow particular buttons for decorations for a block building or for props in dramatic play. Some child may want to practice sewing buttons on cloth items. The special meaning of this visual, tactile material (interesting and fun for adults as well as for children) is its relation to living.

Pieces of cloth These can be cut from old clothing by the teacher or parents; thrift shops and outlet stores are also good sources for obtaining pieces of cloth. Packets of fairly uniform dimensions and variety of fabrics can be used by children in their play activities and in experiences that help them distinguish textures, colors, and patterns and perhaps learn fabric names, such as velvet, cotton, burlap, and wool. It is necessary to observe how a particular group of children responds to such artistically stimulating materials before deciding on the best approaches for storage and use.

Empty thread spools   Tailor shops and parents are sources for this domestic material that can supplement regular classroom construction equipment.   A large bag or basket makes an excellent container for the wooden spools.   The spools may be used for special effect in block building, or if the collection is sufficient, spools may also serve as accessory items for woodworking.

Industrial building materials   Such items are often left over in a building and may be obtained by a teacher or parent who has access to the building.   One of the best materials is floor tiles. Uniform tiles are appealing for children to hold, lay out, fit in various ways, and perceive the effect.   Children can construct floors, paths, borders, or decorations with the tiles.

Special paper   In one school a parent who worked in the printing business contributed discarded wide strips of colored and white heavy paper.   The children used the long pieces of paper to make "long pictures" and experienced a different feeling and process from that of working on paper of usual dimensions.   The children also stapled the long pieces end to end to make them still longer.   How long can a *length* be?   These children were discovering *length* with the aid of some special paper.

Sometimes purchased materials intended for adults can provide artistic activity for preschoolers.   For instance, a hundred colorful spools of thread, fifty different colors or shades of colors, can be ordered from a mail-order house.   Handling, sorting, and arranging such material and talking about it stimulate artistic discrimination, interest, and enjoyment.

Of course, many other kinds of industrial materials are available in each community.   The teacher needs to consider the safety of a material in children's hands, its constructive value, and its appropriateness at a particular time.   Are new materials needed when those in *present* use are still desirable and abundant?   Is there *room* for additions?   Too much material may contribute to fatigue, to distraction, and even to boredom!   The right amount and kind for creative use give children a chance to appreciate the materials, to respect their use, and to have some practical regard for results as well as to derive individual pleasure from the activity.

11 Water, Sand, and Other Natural Materials

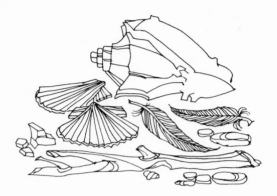

Although there are great abundance and enormous variety of seasonally natural materials that could be useful for artistic activities in a preschool program, adults often overlook them, or pay only slight heed to them. But children, on their own, can be seen working and playing with available natural materials everywhere.

Picking up a stick and making patterns in the dirt is practiced by barefoot village children and by properly attired youngsters wherever they can find dirt underfoot (even in spite of watchful grown-ups.) Children do "dirt drawing" *playfully* and expressively and with the kind of attention that is given to an art form. Dirt drawing is a universal, earthy art form. So is snow stepping, making not only footprints, but also varied impressions in the snow. Perhaps use of natural materials should *precede*, then supplement, and, in some circumstances, substitute manmade art media.

Water in its many forms is available in different quantities and from different sources in any setting. There is water from drizzle and downpour of rain; water drawn from a deep well, from a spigot, or from an unseen source; and reflecting water found in a puddle after rain.

Of the many ways of water play in a preschool program, making bubbles can be described as dazzling! Bubbles have form and color and motion that are altogether brilliant! How easy it is to make them! A child may shake up or vigorously mix water with soap powder, and then blow air through a straw into the suds and see the creation of perfectly spherical bubbles that become delicate airborne objects touched by sun rays, sparkling with colors of the rainbow, varying in size, and multiplying before his eyes. Each child can have a container of soapy water with a straw and create his own gems. The size as well as the shape of the container produces different effects. Children experiment with and discern sizes of bubbles, speed of formation, breath control in blowing, and accumulation of bubbles in particular clusters. They notice how the bubbles adhere, how long they last, and how silently they break! Discovering these characteristics, processes, and changes is actual learning that does indeed proceed from hand to head. A teacher, with the aid of a small illustrated science book, *Soap Bubbles*,[1] can easily interpret facts in response to young children's questions that bubbles generate.

Water is indispensable in providing proper consistency for clay or paints and in serving as an ingredient in play dough. Children begin to sense quantity and the nature of changes that water produces as they use it with various art media.

When Janie saw the teacher adding water to a jar half-filled with thick red paint, she noticed that it resulted in more red paint. How easy to get *more*, Janie must have thought because she promptly put water in two other half-filled paint jars and gleefully proceeded to paint. Her distress was considerable when repeated dippings of the brush did not brighten the paleness of her strokes. Though Janie complained bitterly at first, her complaint turned to challenge as she finally learned from her own experience as well as from the teacher's guidance that she could control the use of water and produce a desired artistic effect.

Walter first *softened* his lump of clay with a few drips of water from a sponge. Next he made his flat "road" shine by dipping his hand in water and smoothing the clay. Then he made the clay mass thinner by wetting it more. Continuing his exploration, Walter made the clay wetter still until it could not be picked up anymore. Walter was fascinated with the changes water could produce!

[1] Seymour Simon. *Soap Bubbles*. New York: Hawthorn Books, Inc., 1969.

Water is also used with other materials in children's improvisations, and the result is a mishmash. A large bowl and a mixing spoon or a beater are needed for this unconventional creative activity. To the water in the bowl a child adds whatever he is allowed: soap, grass, sand, left-over cooking ingredients, dried paints from jars, etc. The process of mixing or integrating each added item and the changes resulting from the additions all seem infinitely absorbing, surprising, and stimulating to the imagination. Five-year-old Scott mixed and whisked various (discarded) real spices with water, then poured the mixture in a tall glass, added a scattering of fresh grass, and "served" it with elegant gestures as "A Toscanini!"

Water in a solid form, too, can be a truly artistic medium for children to explore and to experience. Outdoors they may find underfoot thin, fragile pieces of ice, and they need but little encouragement to look and to hold them, to compare them with glass, to watch them shatter, and to hear them break. In freezing weather it would be easy to freeze water in a shallow pan to produce sheets of glassy ice. Of course, the most brilliant and surprising natural ice creations are *icicles*, hanging, dripping, growing, falling, and crashing from roofs and building ledges in the winter sun. Children notice their formation and transformation and enjoy collecting them, trying even to save them, playing with them, and keeping them in water "so they won't spoil!" If the preschool is in a location that has cold weather in winter, the children can have fun putting limp wet clothes outdoors and seeing them transformed into rigid shapes. For this purpose a few different pieces of clothing from the dress-up supply can be used experimentally. Experience in transformation of form and texture arouses much curiosity, leads to cautious handling, and has bearing on the tactile, visual art as well as on practical knowledge of the natural environment.

Snow, if easily available sometime during the winter months, can provide different sensations, physical contacts, and special delight. Snow offers a unique experience that probably most adults can recall from childhood, though they may no longer share it with children. This pleasure from snow seems deep and individual for each child.

The teacher's role here is, first, to be sympathetic to and patient with children's love of snow and eagerness to have contact with it in many different ways. Second, the teacher gives attention to

proper protective clothing and assures some parents of the goodness and beauty of playing with snow. Third, she provides equipment useful for shoveling snow (perhaps containers for gathering
or packing) and props for enlivening a snow figure.

Usually only older children stay with a snow sculpture long
enough to make a more or less conventional snowman. Younger
preschool children, according to my many years experience,
seem to be irresistibly drawn to breaking the snow figure. This
playful bit of destruction may occur while the child is making
the snowman or while the adult is *supposedly* making it for the
child, or it may happen after either situation. A grown-up may
have difficulty in guarding any kind of snow figure. However,
the adult must remember that for children a snow figure is tempt-
ingly easy to knock down, with no disastrous result, except a
grown-up's disapproval, which can in itself be interesting to the
child. Or, could maybe the large snow figure have some symbolic
and frightening meaning? A teacher may find it interesting to
try to watch unobtrusively preschool children's impulsive, offen-
sive actions against a snowman.

Other snow play involves poking and packing, making impressions in the snow, removing and moving in general handling
of it, discovering its properties, and enjoying its malleability and
changeability. Such actions foster a deep kind of learning and
stimulate artistic sensory responses. Snow play does not result
in conspicious art products that can be uniformly displayed in
windows or taken home or that can elicit praise from relatives.
It does nurture the child's sensibilities and feeling for living.

Sand confined in an outdoor box or a pit is actually one natural
material usually available in preschools. Some nursery schools
and kindergartens even have sandboxes indoors. Too often though
teachers merely tolerate sand play, rather than respect its creative
potential.

A visit to a sandy beach, a sand quarry, or a construction site
where sand is used helps children (and teachers) gain appreciation
of the earthly source and nature of sand. To see a huge quantity
of sand and take some of it in their hands is very impressive to
young children and stimulates imaginative play. If a class trip
to a beach or quarry cannot be arranged, perhaps a teacher or a
parent and a child can visit the place, bring some sand back, and
tell the class about it. Large, vivid, colorful pictures of sandy
areas may be shown to children, too.

In school the teacher needs to observe children's play with sand and to provide appropriate and varied containers and utensils in order to maintain and extend the constructive value of sand play. Children like packing sand and making mounds; therefore, controlled moistening of sand as well as use of differently shaped containers is required. They like transferring sand from one receptacle to another; therefore, a variety of dimensions and capacities among receptacles leads to interesting sand play experiences. For example, getting sand out of a plastic *bottle* with a slim *neck* where flow is somewhat impeded is different from *pouring* it out of a can, *spooning* it out of a bowl, *dumping* it out of a dump truck or box, *shaking* it out of a sifter, or *emptying* it out of a bag or sock! Putting sand *into* all those receptacles has still another kind of appeal and learning.

Some children may be especially interested in using the sandbox for transportation play, such as making roads for trucks or tunnels, if the sand is deep enough. A teacher has to judge what kinds of interests and activities can be provided for in a particular situation and how many children can be accommodated at one time to enable them to explore the sand freely and use it with satisfaction and individual achievement. For some children it may be happy, messy play. For some it might involve serious construction or concentration on weight and volume. For others sand play may mean chatty domesticity with endless "cupcakes" and "birthday cakes" decorated with candles and served with song and ceremony. Sand is a natural material to please that multimedia artist, the preschooler.

Mud is an unconventional, even objectionable, natural material that most young children thoroughly enjoy and quickly find. It provides not only manipulative sensory play, but also sensuous play with heavy pressing, light patting, and apparently pleasurable kneading and slapping motions. If there is no natural mud, such as muddy patches and islands in the yard at certain seasons or after rain, children are likely to say happily, "Let's make some mud!" This very intention is a creative regard for the medium itself. They do not consult a teacher as to technique, for they have never seen her using mud. In fact, they proceed surreptitiously to dig in the dirt in some available spot. Under the guise of "getting a drink" they bring a "spilly" cupful of water and then with poking and stirring (two and sometimes three children) make a delicious mushy substance requiring only their hands — pleasantly muddied hands. This mud play consists of pure sensation, surprising effects, and just plain fun.

At this point a teacher might admit that mud is (unfortunately) attractive to children. Then she may quickly ask: "What's the sense? What could be 'artistic' in mud play especially when there are other, certainly cleaner and more acceptable materials available to everybody?" The answer is self-evident. Mud *is* a universal, earthy play medium and it elicits unmistakable pleasure, both of which are unquestionably healthy for a child. Is there any quarrel with such a premise? Mud play is truly free and freeing play. A child does not engage in mud play to please anyone or to follow any instructions. Mud play might well put the child in a free sensory condition for exploring, enjoying, and creating with more sophisticated materials later.

Mud is also used similarly to clay and sand. Mud can be used imaginatively—becoming "animals" with long tails, "food" stirred diligently with a stick and put in the sun to cook, glossy "pies" decorated with leaves, and muddy "puddings" that look almost real.[2] "Here is some spicing," says Michelle, dropping a few hemlock needles on top of her pudding.

Stones of different sizes that are commonly stumbled upon and cleared away, noticed momentarily and left, or maybe held onto for a while are old and beautiful to see. Stones are rarely considered a distinct, cared-about material to be used in a preschool for playing, for constructing, for creating, and for decorating. Yet, with adult supervision, of course, stones can be a valid and valuable free natural material.

One teacher, spending a summer week in the Finger Lakes country in New York, was attracted by the prevalence of stones that had unusual shapes with dents and even holes. She gathered a heavy, sizable basketful for her nursery school pupils, assuming that they also would be attracted by the stones and that they might use them as block-building accessories. But when she talked about her find to other teachers and friends, they had reservations and offered words of caution: "Not safe; you are asking for trouble. Better not bring them into the classroom! The children will throw them! They won't know what to do with the stones!" However, one or two said, "Try and see."

---

[2] Marjorie Winslow. *Mud Pies and Other Recipes.* New York: The Macmillan Co., 1961.

When the teacher returned to school, she placed a basketful of a selected variety of stones on the shelf with similar basketfuls of block-building accessories. The first children who noticed the stones were advised to take them to a separate area for a better look. Two children and then four removed all the stones, placing them on a table and noticing and naming different shapes: "doughnuts, eggs, turtles," etc. They sorted them according to size; then they made categories of food stones and animal stones. Especially smooth, flat stones seemed right for a driveway near a block building, and others were used for charming decorative effects. Some stones were selected to stay in the housekeeping area as "potatoes." There was no end to ideas for using the stones and a larger supply was clearly in demand. All the children were attracted by the stones and found many opportunities to play with them on the table or on the floor.

Another teacher, noticing some children picking up stones on a class visit to a nearby rocky beach, initiated a rock collection project. The basket she had brought was soon filled, and the children learned through trial and muscular *effort* not only that the basket was filled to capacity in volume, but also that the weight increased to a point where none of the children could budge it and two children together could barely lift it.

Discussion and argument ensued: "Do you want to bring such heavy rocks to school? Why?

"We could build with them outdoors. We could *sit* on the rocks. Take a sunbath. Bring them home for mother's rock garden!"

"Then how would we manage carrying them?"

In response, there was great concentration by the children on figuring out with their own muscle sense which size and weight rocks could be fitted and carried by two children with a grown-up's help. Preference had to be established between big, many, and "nice and smooth." Yes, esthetic value of stones was definitely present.

A teacher who found interest and delight in collecting stones brought to her group of three-year-olds just three solid, heavy, mottled stones and placed them near the water play equipment. The children held them, patted them, rubbed them, and wiped them with wet sponges. Finally they immersed the stones in water in a portable sink, scrubbed them hard with brushes, and then removed and dried them with towels.

"It's beautiful how they play with those stones!" exclaimed the teacher. "Just beautiful!"

Those stones remained as permanent equipment — useful, durable, and "beautiful."

If children's play with stones is not supervised and is ignored by the teacher, stones might become a hazard, in which case they would need to be removed. But when a teacher recognizes the *possibilities* of this natural material, there is much learning and pleasure to be derived from it, as was described in the preceding preschool experiences.

Seashells are avidly collected by people frequenting beaches and are regarded as objects of scientific curiosity and inspiring beauty. No wonder there are so many books about shells! Obviously, shells must be included in the list of natural materials suggested for the preschool program.

What infinite variety of shells there are! So is there a variety of uses for them! If there is a sufficient quantity of small, delicate, glistening shells, children may use them as collage material. If there is a stack of larger, fairly uniform shells, such as sturdy clams or scallops, they can serve as dishes in housekeeping play. An assortment of not too fragile shells kept in an appropriate box can be suitable for a special kind of block building.

A large variety of shells, designated as table material, becomes in the hands and eyes of children a material for intense learning, as I have often observed. When any kind of a shell book with pictures is placed near shells on the table, children usually compare and match the real shells with the pictures. This matching and comparing that involves actual fitting of the shells sometimes onto the pictures, distinguishing not only differences in shape and overall design, but also small details in surface patterns and observing the insideness and outsideness, is really gaining scientific knowledge of shells. Observing such discriminating attention on the part of four-, five-, and six-year-olds, the teacher can enlarge or change the collection to support this intellectual, artistic activity of preschoolers.

Sticks used as natural material provide for sensory learning and experience that have bearing on handling and creating with art media. Sticks when used as learning material should not be any old items like kindling or trash, but deliberately chosen twigs of particular size and thickness collected by the teacher and children. To add importance as well as appeal, the sticks could be held together in manageable bundles (secured with rubber band, wire, or string) and placed in an appropriate box, bag, or basket. Picking up sticks (assuming, of course, sticks are to be found in the vicinity of school) is in itself a natural children's activity which not only gives pleasure, but also sharpens observation and satisfies a collecting proclivity. A common use of this material is construction (so different from cubes and small unit blocks). Sticks make interesting linear designs, vertical enclosures (as with toy logs), "fences" or play trees outdoors or in a sandbox, cargoes for trucks or boats, etc. Since no limit can be placed on imagination, none can be placed on uses of this simple, primitive material handled freely and creatively by young children.

Feathers usually can be found in yards, in parks, near water, at some county or state fairs, on farms, and in other places that wild and domestic birds frequent. If different kinds of feathers are available in the preschool, more creative uses will be found for them. Aside from the children's interest in inspecting and playing with them, feathers have unique practical uses.

Large feathers (from turkey or goose wings) can be made into feather dusters by simply securing a bunch of them with string, wire, or tape. After "dusting" themselves and others, children can actually appreciate the effectiveness of feather dusting of interior surfaces and books. A large, strong feather with a rigid tip makes a real old-fashioned writing quill. Dipping it in ink and scribbling with it is fascinating; the latter action is significantly different from "writing" with a pencil or pen. A rigid feather is excellent for making holes in clay or play dough, for testing doneness of a cake, or making steam holes in a pie. For purely artistic effect feather bouquets can be arranged and rearranged and some feathers can be used as collage material. Still another practical use that children easily understand is making feather pillows. Ripping off the soft parts of feathers and stuffing them in a cloth case is a tedious process. The project may end in making only a doll pillow. Or perhaps a pillow big enough for a child's head can be made from gathered feathers supplemented by feathers from a donated old pillow. In either case, manipulating feathers and investigating their strength, unique lightness, and compressibility certainly stimulate the senses. Nothing else is better for tickling!

Seeds in shells, in pods, and in cases also provide for tactile exploration, for various artistic touches, and for purely pleasant play. What kind of seeds? Here are some examples from my experience. Honey locust trees are fairly common in some cities. Their large, curvy, shiny brown and shaky pods have a curious shape and, when fully ripe, can actually be used as rhythmic shakers. The seeds inside are surprisingly tiny, dark, and smooth and could be used for collages or for housekeeping play. Oaks are common in most parts of the country, and a profusion of capped acorns can be quickly collected. The fit of rough caps on smooth acorns is especially intriguing to children. Leave it to them to put different sizes of acorns to use in some imaginative, dramatic play! Another common tree is the sycamore which produces numerous perfectly round brown balls, hanging like earrings on thin stems. Often these seed balls hang on throughout the winter. How different the countless tightly packed seeds are from the loosely packed locust pods! A collection of sycamore balls can creatively challenge children. Other tightly packed seed containers are the catalpa pods. Seeds are stuffed into the *long*, narrow, green, tough pods which ripen on the trees late in the fall. Quantities of these pods look spectacular and are as inviting to play with as any manufactured materials with educational labels. Delicate, papery, wheat-color pods may be gathered from a mimosa tree.

Balls that look like Christmas decorations, spherical and starry in shape with sharp points, hang from the sweet gum tree. They are fun to gather! A striking kind of seed is the horse chestnut! The outer shell is really rough and prickly and should be touched very lightly and carefully. It has the softest lining and it holds, with exact fit, a perfectly smooth shiny brown nut.

Taking into consideration the fact that children tend to put small objects in their mouths, adults need to be aware of poisonous seeds that come from cultivated and wild plants. Such seeds must be handled cautiously and under supervision. However, avoiding danger need not keep adults and children from knowing, using, and enjoying the endless variety of seeds as well as other natural materials in different parts of the country.

12 Holidays, Celebrations, and Other Occasions

What do holidays of national, historical, religious, or regional nature mean to young children? What can they understand or feel about them? How can holidays be observed interestingly and meaningfully in preschool? Young children after all do not understand history, and they have only vague notions of traditions. However, they sense the general holiday happenings and excitement. They become aware of news and displays of holiday merchandise and the "happy" and the "merry" salutations. Since holidays are an important cultural-social part of community life, they are observed in preschools.

Mrs. Morrow, a nursery school teacher, was eager to inform the children of historical events of Thanksgiving. She reasoned that since the children sat still for story time, and responded to picture books, she could hold their attention with a Thanksgiving story. She also believed that a spirit of thankfulness should be inculcated early, and she should use her teacher authority in this respect.

When the friendly Mrs. Morrow called for story time, the children ran toward and around her like chicks. The children soon settled in a routine circle, offering bits of different news which the teacher acknowledged. Then she indicated they must listen to her. She showed them pictures of Pilgrims, and the children commented on the costumes, but the strange word *Pilgrims* made no impression. Mrs. Morrow explained how hard the Pilgrims worked building houses and planting food. Although the children's attention to Mrs. Morrow was friendly, there was no appearance of comprehension. For them building houses probably meant their kind of "block construction" and "planting food" could have meant emptying shopping bags onto pantry shelves, an experience these suburban children knew. Mrs. Morrow was disappointed that her story did not capture the interest of this "bright" group as it *had* the previous kindergarten class. She turned then to the aspect of thankfulness, asking the children what they were thankful for, to which different ones responded.

"I say 'thank you.' "

"And 'please' too.' "

"You have to say 'you are welcome.' "

Obviously, the children were not thinking of the meaning of thankfulness per se as the teacher *wanted*. Mrs. Morrow had such good and definite intentions that became marred by frustration.

"You must be thankful for all the good things your mommies and daddies give you," she declared.

No doubt Mrs. Morrow had in mind parents' desire as well as her own to have such a lesson emphasized.

". . . good things," a child echoed, picking out from the teacher's lesson a phrase that was meaningful to him.

Happily for all, Mrs. Morrow not only showed magazine pictures of good things to eat for Thanksgiving dinner but also several real root vegetables for the children to handle. She was pleased with the children's interest in the vegetables as they were picking up and rubbing and sniffing them. However, she recognized that their "yum-yum" reaction to Thanksgiving dinner had no deeper meaning.

To many children Thanksgiving means happy family reunions, acquaintance with relatives, and a splendid dinner. This important social and personal experience for the child can be shared in school by informal talking and preparation and eating of particular foods. Such an approach is most wholesome and understandable for children. It can lead into other experiences that present new information.

What happened in school on Lincoln's birthday celebration as reported in Chapter 10? First came the familiar happy birthday song which introduced more and different music. Then in response to children's interest in Lincoln, the teacher showed pictures and answered questions related to his life. But if Lincoln's death had been queried, the teacher would have answered accurately the historical fact of assassination.

One American figure about whom children learn early in school is George Washington. In celebration of his birthday they learn the usual cliché of referring to him as "the father of our country" and some learn to draw uniform, standard pictures of cherry trees and hatchets. Children get a notion, too, that George Washington was *greatness* and *goodness*, totally and unquestionably. But some teachers and schools are venturing into broader knowledge of history for themselves. As a result, they try to present concrete, practical (rather than patriotic) history; for instance: "George Washington was the *first* president; people voted for him. People remember him now with statues and monuments. Cities, bridges, schools, and other people are named after him." This information can be appreciated by children, for this is living history. The fact that George Washington was a well-to-do man and, legitimately in his time, owned slaves may come up and prove a provocative subject for five- or six-year-olds. In such a discussion the teacher might get from the children ideas that suggest other activities and experiences that need to be provided.

The same principle of concrete information applies to birthday celebrations of Martin Luther King, who achieved historical fame in his short lifetime. A school in any town or community that observes his birthday would plan some observance for young children. Available photographs of Dr. King leading people on marches and delivering impassioned speeches are certainly impressive and are likely to inspire comments and questions. The teacher who cares needs to understand the social convictions and actions that brought Martin Luther King to leadership. From her own understanding she distills something relevant and positive for the children.

Children associate holidays with traditional food: Christmas candies, Valentine cakes, painted eggs for Easter, etc. There are special ethnic holiday foods; for example: matzos for the Jewish Passover, fruity panettone loaves that are traditional Italian, and round moon cakes with sweet fillings prepared by

the Chinese for the Moon Festival. In the spirit of holiday sharing, different traditional foods can be enjoyed informally by
teachers and children.

With the class a teacher may prepare some foods for holiday
celebrations even if no other cooking is attempted throughout
the year.

"We made Santa Claus cookies for Christmas!" Richie told
his mother. "They are real! Smell them!"

On the table he emptied a plastic bag of cookies shaped like
Santa Claus. He also showed the cookies to relatives and friends
who came to the house.

Although the teacher used prepared cookie dough ("to avoid
a mess") which limited Richie's experience, and although she
used only one kind of cookie cutter ("to avoid confusion of children having to choose") that made Richie's involvement somewhat superficial, still he did press the cutter into the dough. Thus,
he had a small *hand* in the project and he brought home something special and tangible for *that* holiday. Taking part, even
though a very small part, in making the cookies in class gave
Richie a sense of personally observing the holiday.

In another class, holiday food was also prepared by the children but with a different kind of teacher planning and guidance.
They made cranberry relish from a recipe supplied by a mother
who worked with half of the class. (The other half had their turn
the next day.) This was a messy job indeed! The messiness itself was enjoyed by the children and was accepted by the adults
because (without saying it) they accepted children's interest in
handling raw materials. The group ground and mashed the slippery
cranberries and oranges, poured sugar, and counted and identified
each child's container which was to be taken home. Different
operations went on simultaneously and this activity appeared somewhat chaotic. However, judging by the facial expressions and
sounds, all the licking and "lip smacking" and comments of holiday anticipation about when the relish would be eaten showed
happy, memorable involvement with holiday preparation.

Children, basically, have no religious prejudice, so holiday
foods and toys are interesting *in themselves*. David brought a
dreidel to nursery school and no one knew what it was, not even
the teacher. All were fascinated by the toy and wanted to play
with it (as they would want to play with a spinning top). They
learned not only the word *dreidel* but also something about

Hanukkah. The teacher contacted David's family for advice on purchasing a few dreidels to add to the enjoyment of the holiday. This was an impressive way for the Christian children (who were in majority in the class) to become acquainted with the Jewish child and for the latter to make a contribution!

A Mexican piñata for a class Christmas party would provide special gaiety and humor. The Mexican child or an invited Mexican adult could contribute to the occasion and take a very active part in it.

One of the most beautiful holiday traditions that is especially appealing to children everywhere is decorating and lighting an evergreen tree. The presence of a real tree in their midst is a unique pleasure for young children, and their participation in hanging the decorations gives them a sense of relation to the tree.

Although decorating an evergreen is generally recognized as a Christian ritual in this country, it is as much a folk and family tradition. Some people may contend that a Christmas tree in the classroom is unfair Christian indoctrination of non-Christians or nonbelievers. If the teacher's aim is to provide a social and esthetic experience that is enriching and enjoyable for all children, there is no religious emphasis intended or given.

There are celebrations which do not appear on the calendar, but which constitute regional, national, or international observances. For instance, the two hundredth birthday of the composer Ludwig van Beethoven was observed in 1970 and referred to in the mass media over a period of months. This occasion provided a wonderful opportunity for all children to become acquainted with some of Beethoven's music. Such a celebration, of course, depends on the teacher's musical taste and interest. She may find recorded selections of his lighter music for the children to dance to or expressive mood music for accompaniment to art work or for listening at rest time. She may also bring in interesting pictures.

Centennial celebrations of the founding of a town or city may begin with children's dramatizations of the event. Also, children may engage in activities related to celebrations of important local structures. For example, Brooklyn Bridge had a gala eighty-eighth birthday in 1971. What would be more appealing to children than to celebrate the birthday of a bridge with a visit to the bridge to see and "feel" its size and majesty and to discuss its strength and solidity! Then what could be more knowing for children than to have a *hand* in *experimenting* with the construction of a bridge with blocks and other media!

An unusual celebration took place recently in New York State. A printed local announcement read: "You are invited to the dedication of a landmark, Putnam County's Oldest Tree, a majestic white oak at the site of an Indian camp ground." The celebration included Indian dancing, impressive statements on the long life (about three hundred years) of the white oak and the present protection given it, and the ceremonious unveiling of a plaque. Many children of all ages came to the celebration, taking away with them pictures of the white oak. What an unusual opportunity for young children and teachers in the nearby communities to display pictures and to encourage creative expression in honor of a distinguished neighbor, the white oak.

Various weekly celebrations throughout the nation might well interest young children—Brotherhood Week, for instance. What is brotherhood? Can sisters be in it, too? What can you make for Brotherhood Week? Whom do you want for a brother? Such explorations of *brotherhood* can be meaningful to five-year-olds and some four-year-olds.

A celebration of Earth Day or Earth Week is certainly concrete and "down-to-earth" and, therefore, understandable to young children. Earth is something they are very close to in more than the literal sense. It is easy enough to elicit their appreciation of earth because they can respond not only in words, but also in action: living on the earth, playing on it, digging and planting in it, and eating what it brings forth. Earth Day is earth *protection*, protection from trash and poisons. Thus, Earth Week is "to walk and look around the class, school, block, street, and alley." The discerning children will meet such challenge, notice the trouble, and figure out what to do about clearing, cleaning, and using (instead of wasting) so that living on the earth is enjoyable. Here then is an occasion for active children to try with adults to be philosophical, scientific, practical, and poetic and for teachers to work on continuity of interest in the physical environment.

The greatest celebration for naturally egocentric preschoolers is their own birthday. This should not be taken for granted or attended to in a routine fashion by adults. Since a child's birthday is intensely important to him, for on this day he legitimately, publicly, and happily celebrates himself, an elaborate party with lots of presents is unnecessary. What *is* important is the distinction of the day. The teacher should have advance knowledge of the day, mark it clearly on the calendar for all to see, and personally call the birthday child's attention to it. *Assurance* of the celebration matters more to the young child than surprise. He is happy to know that the teacher and mother prepared the cake and special drink (perhaps juice out of small bottles with colorful straws, instead of out of the usual paper cups). In some communities there are customs for children's birthdays, such as expensive presents or favors for the class, or prescribed decorations that have to be bought. Some parents insist on observing these customs because they want to feel that they are doing right by their child so that they do not incur any criticism. But even these parents can learn that a simpler personal celebration touches the heart of the birthday child and creates a spirit of celebration that does not escape him or his class.

Crude but colorful decorations such as children's crayon drawings that serve as individual mats or tablecloth add to the festive air and symbolize a birthday party. A unique teacher-made paper crown for the particular child or a bright ribbon tied only on his chair signifies that he is being distinguished. The resulting expression on his face shows how "great" he feels. Such simple props plus a cupcake for each child and the birthday child's lighted with candles, the teacher's personal attention, and perhaps a guest invited by the child make the birthday important and happy for him.

When there is such a celebration, the other children are hardly able to wait for their birthdays to come. Occasionally, a child is so desirous of a celebration for himself that he snatches the birthday ribbon to attach to *his* chair. Others say earnestly, "I want my birthday to be now!" A teacher does not just say, "Don't be silly," and thus slight their frustration and impatience. Such feelings are hard to live through for some children, even for those older than preschoolers. The teacher must be observant of and sympathetic to children with such sensitive egos.

Celebrations of known holidays and expected occasions require planning and involvement of children in the preparations. A teacher may obtain help from parents in advance so that changes in routines can be managed smoothly and the celebration can take place impressively or perhaps can occur expeditiously.

However, unexpected happenings may require change of plans and bring disruption to comfortable routines. A change of mood in the teacher, children, and class atmosphere can be effected by an unexpected happening such as school property damage due to vandalism. How does a teacher handle such a situation? Does she dismiss it or talk her way through it so as not to "disrupt the class"? How does she handle her own and the children's concrete personal responses?

A nursery school teacher of a private school walked into her classroom one Monday morning together with a group of children who had arrived early, and beheld with horror a broken window and glass strewn all over the otherwise clean and well-prepared room. But in spite of the shock and distress the teacher did not overlook the children and their impression and interest. The teacher felt she should have the children take part in the problem all the way. Physical safety was, of course, the first concern, and the teacher indicated the small area in the room and the hall which the children could occupy. That was understandable to them. Second, proper report of the accident and immediate help had to be obtained. "Tell the office," suggested Larry. The teacher sent a note with three children, which resulted in having the secretary and another teacher come in with a large broom. Two of the children served as guards, telling all the arrivals not to go into the "dangerous" place until the adults finished the sweeping. Then the children were assigned to a job of being "inspectors." They examined with closest attention every area for "small, almost invisible specks of glass." Then they realized the room was too cold, and the teacher told them that a man would come in later to fix the broken window.

"But can't we cover up the hole now?" After some discussion and searching for a board, the hole was covered with a piece of cardboard; so the problem of physical safety and protection was attended to with sufficient understanding and with security for the children. The teacher had gained cooperation from the children easily enough in a moment of need; they had also shown responsibility and given necessary help. But the episode led to the serious question of cause, which in turn led to the moral issue of wrong doing which was involved in the broken window.

"How did the window get broken?" several children asked of the teacher right away.

"I am not sure. Have you any idea?" Fantastic answers of jets and bombs and flying saucers came from those four- to five-year-olds, showing what children are thinking about. Some thought the break came from a ball.

"Maybe a boy was playing and he didn't *know* the ball was going to hit the window." Consideration of cause brought to mind responsibility and the possibility of someone's guilt.

"Maybe a bigger boy did it."

"I didn't do it." This was said very seriously and a hush of consternation settled over the group of children.

"I know you didn't," the teacher said confidently, relieving the hush.

"Maybe a pussycat did!" This child wanted to be funny and succeeded. Everybody laughed and made pawing motions of breaking a window. The laughter and movement served to relieve the children's tension. Then a little girl said, "Whoever did it, should clean up."

"But it's already cleaned up." They were thus back to the concrete solution and the teacher ended it at this point.*

The teacher could have kept the children in another classroom while their room was being cleaned and then proceeded with the daily program as planned. But the opportunity for the children to respond to the minor disaster and do something about their own damaged room gave the children and the teacher a chance to carry out responsibilities together and to reflect sensibly on "crime" and consequences.

Another unfortunate happening that can disrupt routines and even cause some trauma is an accident to a child. A hurt child and the emergency treatment he may need require immediate action from the teacher. Simultaneously, concerned attention should be given to the frightened child who might have caused the hurt deliberately or inadvertently. Honest reassurance has to be provided for the other children who might have become frightened and confused or even panicky at the sight of blood or the sound of a scream. This situation is where the teacher's human response to someone else's hurt and her adult responsibility and equilibrium come into action. She has to look at the hurt child without panic and to apprise the parents or the doctor as accurately as possible of the nature of the accident. She must be willing (and this is probably the hardest part) to share with the children both her knowledge and her concern.

"The blood is from the cut on the front of the head, not the eyes," the teacher quietly told her class. "And the doctor will put stitches in the cut, he'll sew it up. . . . Yes, it does hurt a lot. Linda's mother is on the way now to take her to the doctor, and I'll stay with her till then, quietly in the hall, so she'll feel better,

*From: Kindergarten: A Year of Learning by Marguerita Rudolph and Dorothy H. Cohen. Copyright © 1964 by Meredith Publishing Company. By permission of Appleton-Century-Crofts, Educational Division, Meredith Corporation, pp. 347–348.

and I'll hold this cloth over the cut. . . . Well, you and Mrs. Rogers will manage in the class without me for a while."

The children rose to the occasion by being cooperative and helpful. When Linda wanted water, several of them rushed to get it.

As Linda and her mother were leaving for the doctor's office nearby, the teacher encouraged them to stop in class on their way home so that the children could see Linda after she had received medical attention. Linda and her mother returned to the school and were pleased, perhaps even proud, with the sympathetic attention from the classmates. The children, after looking Linda over and touching her, were convinced that the doctor did fix the cut successfully and that Linda was safe and sound. The implication to each child was personal: "When I hurt, my teacher will take care of me as she did of Linda. Mother will come. The doctor will fix the hurt. My friends will be nice to me."

While sledding with his family, Paul suffered a broken shinbone. At the hospital a rigid, clumsy looking cast was put on his leg. He bore the pain and discomfort as well as the surgical mechanics not only with courage, but also with interest, observing all details. Although having an immobilized child in a crowded classroom with sixteen active preschoolers would require considerable patience and serious responsibility on the part of the teacher, she together with the parents (and Paul) agreed that Paul should come to school. They believed that the experiences of accommodating Paul and of learning firsthand about broken bones, tough casts, and recovery progress would be valuable for the children. They also felt that the cheerful atmosphere in the busy room with different appealing hand activities would hasten Paul's recovery. The mother was willing to carry him up the stairs to the room where Paul could then move around on the imposing looking crutches. All that trouble was worth it because, though Paul had become "broken" and immobilized, he was still accepted in class by loyal friends and teacher.

More serious situations can also happen in a preschool setting. At such times, too, the teacher cannot hide facts and avoid dealing with them. One of my most profound experiences was the death of one of the children at home.[1]

[1] Marguerita Rudolph. "Should the Children Know." In *Women's Home Companion*, Aug. 1952.

Having learned of the tragedy directly from the mother, I expressed my own feelings of grief by attending Rachael's funeral. Then, with my Director I discussed what I should tell the children. The Director decided it was vital to consult with all the parents in order to learn how *they* felt and what they wished to tell their children. All the parents responded by coming to a meeting held at school. All had deep sympathy for Rachael's parents and all naturally were protective toward their own young, instinctively desirous of *shielding* their children from the *knowledge* of Rachael's death. They believed, or perhaps *wanted* to believe, that this was possible. Different ones commented, "Tell the children Rachael's family moved out of town." "Rachael is going to another school." A clergyman among the parents advised seriously to tell the children not that Rachael had died, but that "she had gone to Heaven where she is happy." Many parents agreed with that because their attitude was: "Tell the children anything as long as the actual tragic facts of death were not disclosed to them." The parents were not in a position to give rational thought to children's education, but I had the educational responsibility. I had to communicate my thoughts and intentions to the parents in such a way that would be meaningful to them. I had to state concretely what was appropriate learning from life for their children. Though differently from the parents, I *cared* about all the children. By this time of the year I knew what they were like and what kind of rapport I had with them. It would be impossible, I explained to the parents, either to conceal or to lie *about something so important* to the children and to me. Children read inner feelings, especially negative ones, and somehow they know by the voice, by a facial expression, or perhaps by the *unsaid* thoughts that something important has taken place. I explained that although parents at home may avoid mentioning death or may find comfort in referring to Heaven, I would quietly and at an appropriate time in class discuss the subject and let the children *talk* about Rachael's death so that I could tell what they knew or what they feared. I could find out how they felt and what reassurances or answers I or the parents might need to give them. I told the parents that I had to follow the dictates of my conscience and my educational responsibility. The parents understood, or perhaps just believed me, and agreed with my plan.

The other teachers in the school as well as parents were interested and learned a great deal from the children's thoughtful, practical, and always deeply human expressions. Yes, the four-year-olds had some knowledge of death already.

"Well," said one, "my granny is *already* in the hospital."

"When my grandma died, grandpa got himself another wife," another child noted.

"Did the mother cry?" a little girl asked, indicating concern with grief for the living.

Many questions and comments had to do with the cause of Rachael's death and causes of death in general. The seriousness of this discussion, though it was brief, was apparently too heavy for the children to bear and they spontaneously turned to humor. They began enumerating absurd objects that may be swallowed (and cause death) and they laughed with obvious relief, rather similarly to the children's laughter in the vandalism episode. When the answer to their question "Will she come alive again?" was "No," one child resolved to avoid death altogether.

"I am never going to die!" he proclaimed and no one contradicted him.

Then one child even thought of a personal advantage that may accrue from another's death.

"My baby brother died," he said, referring to his resented, living rival.

Also, there was a note of spiritual regard for the dead when one child suggested: "Don't cross Rachael's name off so we'll remember her."

Not all the children could talk about Rachael's death. One child, although he had the same opportunity as the others, did not say anything and he was not urged or questioned. He said nothing at home either and had nightmares for a few nights. Then toward the end of the year he made some vague statements about the death and talked to the teacher. An opportunity for children *to talk meaningfully and freely* when experiencing stress, sudden trouble, and trauma is enormously helpful to all.

A newspaper report relating to the 1971 California earthquake dealt with psychic disturbances the quake caused as studied by the San Fernando Valley Child Guidance Clinic.

. . . The best therapy, psychiatrists agree, is to talk about one's fears. Dr. Stephen Howard suggested that planning for future disasters include mental health services.

"The Red Cross has 'Keep a Stiff Upper Lip' attitude. That's the way they maintain peace and control," he explained. "They urged people not to talk about the earthquake. But from a mental health point of view, if you don't talk about it, your anxieties get all pent up, and it's much worse."*

Because of the close personal regard the teacher must have for each child and indirectly for his family, she needs to be apprised of *any* tragic family happening. For whether the child remains quiet and *appears* unaffected or is conspiciously upset, he may suffer from the disturbance. In such a case, the teacher's friendly availability without forced commiseration and the teacher's informal sharing of her understanding with the other children might elicit natural expression of grief and give comfort and help to the child.

Another disruption and change of classroom program and curriculum may come from a community event that affects children. For instance, there was a milk strike one year during which milk deliveries were curtailed or stopped for a whole week. In one preschool, the teacher explored available milk products that might serve as substitutes for milk. The strike situation stimulated new interest and added to the teacher's and the children's knowledge about milk and milk products, as well as brought about greater appetite for dairy foods.

In another kind of a strike, questions and discussion in kindergarten turned to real economics: What is a strike? A kind of fight when workers want something they are not getting from the boss. Who are the strikers? They are real, otherwise peaceful people, not just fighters. (One child seemed to think strikers went around physically striking others.) What will happen? A settlement will come. It means the fighting sides will *make up* and the workers will get something and return to work. The boss will give something and go back to being in charge. Wages? When you work *for* somebody and somebody pays you money.

Talking with children about happenings requires thinking about essentials and speaking honestly in understandable language. But whether the happening is world news such as men landing on the moon, or a natural disaster such as a flood, there are still the questions: How much should the teacher control discussion? How much information should she contribute? Should she try to influence children?

After John F. Kennedy's assassination a teacher brought in

*From "Coast Quake Left Psychic Tremors" by Steven V. Roberts. In *The New York Times*, Mar. 6, 1971.

a photograph of him as an expression of her own emotional reaction. Many children knew the likeness of the president and made disconnected comments about the tragedy. Because of her own feeling of involvement, the teacher brought in a magazine picture of the funeral.

She said to a few children who came to look, "All those people and many others are very sad that President Kennedy was killed."

"Are you sad?" a child asked the teacher in a reflective manner.

Other children commented on having seen the funeral on television and spoke of their parents being sad.

"My mother cried," another child said.

Then, absorbing the mood, a child said slowly and quietly: "I am sad, too."

"I know," said the teacher, restraining herself from further emotional expression.

Then a spontaneous, true moment of silence in the classroom followed, as though everyone sensed that words and noise would spoil the feeling and the respect. Quickly, though it seemed casually, the children returned to the business at hand. The teacher did not leave the funeral picture in class but left the Kennedy portrait, which she removed at the usual time for changing pictures.

Some significant events bring out children's powers of description if they have an opportunity and incentive to talk. The day after the big blackout, the electric power failure in the northeast, the children talked excitedly about the unusual occurrences.

"My daddy couldn't come home—the subway didn't go."

"The elevators didn't work."

"We lighted candles!"

But one child gave this personal account: "My father said 'Damn it!' My mother started to cry, and my brother wet his pants."

Since the news of the blackout was reported nationally, a five-year-old girl in the South had a story for her class the next day.

"I read in the newspaper," she said (a nonreader, putting on an air of authenticity), "that there was a . . ." She couldn't remember the strange term, but thoroughly understood the meaning and so supplied a description, ". . . there was a *light-out* in New York."

Events come and go and whatever the unusual experience has been, the group of children and adults will surely return to familiar routines with a fresh view or changed attitude and with added knowledge and enriched language.

13 The Threshold of Literacy

Although *preschool* is generally regarded, at least partially, as *school*, there is a significant difference. A traditional school is thought of as a place where children are trained in literacy and are taught subjects, where teaching is usually separate from life and play, where teachers must be in control of children, and where children are expected to be obedient. As indicated in innumerable studies and official reports, preschool should *not* be school. The educational purpose of a preschool is not attainment of literacy, but rather participation in living and practical learning which promotes individual growth in an atmosphere of security and acceptance.

Various devices are often placed conspicuously in some preschools to proclaim the high esteem in which literacy is held by the adults. Walls of classrooms are often dominated by a permanently affixed alphabet, printed color charts, or a standard chart of shapes. These devices command unquestionable respect from the adults, whether they are used on a regular basis or once in a while to prod and probe children's "readiness." The usual answer to the question of the purpose of such formal items is: "The alphabet and charts are there only for the children who are ready to learn; we don't force the others." This implication seems to be that learning is equated with formal attainment in school subjects. Generally, children who catch on to reading are automatically judged to be superior to others and are given special attention to further promote *school* skills. Meanwhile significant *preschool* practices and achievements are not given equal respect and attention, and the preschool child's basic needs for growth and learning go unmet.

Some preschools not only display silent symbols of striving for literacy, but also conduct "experimental" instructional programs in reading and writing. General rationales for such programs are that the children have this instruction *no more than* twenty minutes three times a week, and that the programs will be discontinued if proved ineffective. The implication here is that preschool children still have the greatest portion of time for other activities and play. It is obvious, however, that once funds and professional prestige are invested, there are pressures and rationalizations to continue the instruction even if it bores and oppresses many children.

Still other preschools, disclaiming any resemblance to school in their program, actively strive to prepare children for school life by emphasizing *school behavior* during the whole year. Such accomplishments as the following are held in high esteem: *raising the hand* before speaking in a group, even though the group is small and hand raising is an obstacle to free expression, and some young children resort to hand raising purely for exercise; *using correct* (conventional) *speech* which the teacher praises *loudly* (for example, when a child says, "May I?") while indirectly criticizing others; *forming a straight line* in various unnecessary situations which are *likely* to irritate young children or provoke mischievous behavior; and *being quiet.* The thinking that favors such accomplishments is that when children enter school later it will not be a painful shock for them to give up indulgences and kindnesses of a preschool and to conform to school behavior. It would be unfair, therefore, to preschool children not to teach them the basics of school behavior, for presumably without this knowledge school learning cannot proceed smoothly. It seems then that the teacher does not hold such school behavior as "right" for *preschoolers,* but she is obligated to *prepare* children for success in school. When are the powers, pleasures, and unique opportunities of the preschool years to be enjoyed?

The teacher's responsibility is to assess the total preschool environment to which the young child relates and to determine how it does meet his needs for learning and how *this learning* brings him to an inviting threshold of literacy. In the preschool room there should be attractive books which a child can hold in his own hands, which he approaches and handles with curiosity and interest, and which a teacher shares pleasurably with him and with the other children. There should be useful labels with mysterious markings which his keen eye detects and discovers mean his name—himself. At the same time, in the course of the child's experiences he encounters other meaningful markings— signs in his environment: "This piece of wood with letters says you can't go on this road. The *sign* tells you not to go there— that's how you know. Other letters on a white paper bag tell you it's flour."

In his class the child can *figure out* what is important for him to know. Jessie saw some juicy red cherries in the bowl.

"Are they for *all* the children?" she asked, surveying all the faces (or maybe all the mouths). "Will *I* get some, too?"

Though the answer was Yes, Jessie looked thoughtful, then decided to sit next to the bowl in order to be closest to *reach* into it. Thus, Jessie may not have been learning numbers or doing verbal counting, but she recognized a problem that mattered to her, and she calculated the approach to its solution.

In spontaneous play and use of materials preschool children show the knowledge and skills which lead to the threshold of literacy. Absorbed in doing a puzzle, for instance, a child looks at, studies, and fits the shapes as he learns how separate pieces become a whole. He turns one shape on all sides until he *knows* it is in the *right* place. He has an unmistakable look of success and might actually say, "I did it." Likely as not, though, he *says* nothing. Right after completing the puzzle, he may flop it upside down on the table and start all over again to feel that sweet taste of completion and of success. On his own, he is likely to practice diligently doing the same puzzle for days until the coordination, the seeing, the judging, and the fitting acts are mastered. He is then ready for a new challenge, perhaps a more complex puzzle with more pieces which would bring that feeling of success.

Another common item among standard preschool supplies is a pegboard and pegs. Young preschoolers engage in attentive manipulation of the pegs and creation of individual patterns within confines of the board. Also they find satisfaction in performing a mechanical task of sticking a peg in each hole, line by line horizontally, left to right, right to left, vertically, or even from corner to corner, with either no regard for color or carefully selecting and using one color of pegs at a time. Sometimes a child makes a pattern with the pegs without covering all the holes in the board. After vigorous outdoor play young children actually like to sit down for awhile and engage in some quiet manipulative activity that affords individual learning of color discrimination, of making a directional pattern, of handling quantities and inadvertently being stimulated to count, yet not having to *account* for the result, pleasing only themselves with quick gain of skill and independent work. Such pleasant, simple tasks give a child confidence to tackle more complicated and challenging tasks.

When children engage in block building, there is often great involvement of brawn and brain, excitement, urgent problems to overcome, and daring solutions to try. Bang! A child brings a big pile of heavy blocks, uses floor space around, and clink-clank erects a structure with four sides. He can put himself inside and can step out before building himself in! He may also enjoy having the help of co-workers who have ideas, too, and get pleasure from the building.

"Oh boy! Look at this garage!" said George who seemed to think all he had to do next was to put on the roof.

According to his quick eye survey, this would be easy.

"But what's this?" he thought. "How odd! Roof blocks the same size as walls don't fit; they keep falling in."

"I know, we'll get longer blocks!" he exclaimed.

Acting on his own decision resulted in great satisfaction. Yes, the longer blocks did cover the open top of the garage.

"There's the roof . . . oh-oh!" shouted one co-worker.

One end of the roof tipped.

"Move it the other way," George reasoned.

There was balance to attain, there was size to take into account, and there was distinction to be made between one side of the roof and the other. The teacher nearby saw how precarious the roof still was and wanted to advise George and his co-workers. But seeing *their satisfaction*, she did not want to interfere.

"It worked!" the three builders shouted, jubilant with their roof.

But their joy was quickly replaced by another frustration.

"How can the cars get in?" one asked.

Alas, the garage was built and sealed on all sides.

"Those poor kids," the teacher thought. "That's too much frustration. I've got to help them. This would be the right time."

Wrong! As soon as she bent down and started pointing to a possible solution, there were angry rebuffs and threatening gestures with a block! What a letdown to have someone else finish their important job! No! Their *own* solution would be better in spite of any difficulty. The children did *figure out* (there on the spot) that removing two blocks provided, if not a door that could be moved, at least a passage for cars to roll in and out of the garage. What *cautious* manipulation and *steady hand* the removal of those blocks required! "Admirable," the teacher had to admit, getting over her injured pride at seeing her judgment and help being rejected.

Children's learning must reflect their own temperament as well as their special interest in trying out ideas and "doing their own thing." Then such skills as estimating dimensions, assessing position, recognizing balance, and discovering how to make adjustments become important and are learned. These skills are not only cognitive, but also muscular, sensory, and personal — characteristic of preschool learning.

A six-year-old boy declined to read a book that his remedial teacher placed before him. He expressed a preference for a "better" story which the teacher would read *to him* and she complied. When he was offered an arithmetic page to do, he attacked it with vigor! He liked writing numerals, especially big ones. He was conscious not only of forming them as he jotted each numeral with a slight jerk of the pencil, but also of the *sense* the symbols made to him. As he wrote correctly by tens, from top to bottom on the paper, he made each numeral bigger in size than the preceding one. The teacher looked askance as she mentioned the size of the written numerals, but her voice was kindly, almost indulgent, because after all he was "immature." The child paid no heed to her suggestion that all symbols should be written the same size, and when he wrote the triumphant numeral 100, he made it powerful by comparison to the others. He could not fit the big 100 on the one page so he completed it, naturally, by putting one zero on the other side. According to his logic, 100 had a right to be the biggest in size, and the suggestion that all numerals be the same made no sense. The teacher, however, seemed to overlook the child's sense about numbers as well as his originality. Or, did she perhaps believe that such sense and originality would interfere with school learning?

Adults are often obsessed with the value of language per se and unintentionally misjudge and confuse young children. When a child talks a lot, he is described as *outgoing*. When he uses phrases pleasing to adult ears, the adult is *proud* of his words. On the other hand, a child is criticized for being *shy* when he has the dignity not to answer a grown-up stranger who demands to know his name.

Larry's parents were proud of his vocabulary. One day in his nursery class Larry had such fun whacking another child on the head, saying "I am sorry," and going on to the next classmate, with a whack, and "I am sorry." This fun, of course, was followed by distress and hollering from the innocents.

"What's going on here?" questioned the surprised teacher.

Larry was surprised by the disapproving tone, and promptly answered with cultivated clarity, "I *said* 'I am sorry.' "

Then, having paid his verbal admission, he was ready to proceed with the fun of whacking one classmate after another. Apparently Larry had learned precociously from adults that correct words matter in social interaction. But there was a reaction from one of his next victims, Laura, who unhesitatingly returned what had been given her twofold, and she did this with no words of accompaniment. Larry was stunned momentarily into silence and then became very expressive with a hefty holler. From this incident Larry learned from a child that deeds matter more than words.

Sometimes when a child acquires speech, it is assumed that his childish utterances have a grown-up value. When children simply memorize words and verbal information, teachers commend them for being knowledgeable or smart. Also, young children's imitation of grown-up words and gestures is often equated with mature attitudes.

A school official showed a visitor a kindergarten class performing the daily ceremony of pledging allegiance to the flag.

"I want you to watch that kid in the blue shirt. See how he turns his head and holds his hand on his chest and enunciates the words. That's what I call *patriotism!*" the official noted with pride.

In a recent television advertisement, a company that produces remedial reading kits showed children no older than six years who were uttering half words, stumbling, stammering, and being silent with embarrassment, while trying to recite the Pledge. For some viewers, this ad might have indicated that the children had a language problem! Does inability to recite words that are difficult, abstract, and meaningless for young children really indicate language deficiency? Or, does it show the inappropriateness of the task?

An equally common misjudgment of the role of children's language is the assumption that when children are quiet they are automatically *nice, polite,* or *attentive* (especially if they are quiet when a grown-up speaks).

"You are not listening," the teacher told Ann who asked a question when the teacher was reading.

But Aaron who was concentrating on pulling a shoelace out of his shoe was judged to be listening.

"Now boys and girls," said the school librarian to the kindergarten children, "remember what the library rule is!" She continued to admonish them in advance. "And *show me* how quiet you can be," as though she thought "Be quiet for *my* sake; do it to please me."

But twenty or more five-year-olds sitting at big tables in close proximity cannot be still for long. Often a book slips, a pencil falls, somebody pushes. A crowd of sociable, friendly children (although holding on to chosen picture books) naturally look at one another and exchange confidences and teasers.

Inevitably they elicit disapproval from the librarian: "I am very disappointed in you, boys and girls. I thought you had learned about library behavior by now. Your teacher told me you were so grown-up. And now what will I say to her?"

The librarian no doubt meant "You behave for your teacher's sake." She thus elicited the desired *external* composure.

How *brave* must the child be who seeks a way out of imposed quietness, actually resisting the brainwashing!

One day an elementary school principal met a group of nursery school children who had come with their teacher to visit the kindergarten which they would attend the next term. He had come out of his office especially to greet them in the school corridor.

"Good morning, boys and girls! How do you like our *nice quiet* school? Now remember, when you are going to come to kindergarten next fall, *you* are going to be nice and quiet, too."

The children were indeed impressed with the principal's words and stood and stared for a moment in silence. But one irrepressible four-year-old broke through the silence: "I am going to be in the second grade." (Safe distance away from the quiet kindergarten, he figured.)*

Clearly, the child understood the principal only too well! But did the principal understand the child?

The preceding accounts clearly indicate that a preschool program needs to be *broadly* educational and that children's skills bearing on literacy must be part of their *total* pursuit. The teacher cannot think of a young child's educational potential as something separate to be measured and coded. Instead she must consider the reality of the whole child, responding, appreciating, and living with him so that some knowledge and feeling about him results in effective and meaningful action. One spontaneous demonstration can be more telling than any devised (and often misleading) test.

Three-year-old Nicky's vocabulary included numbers, and occasionally he was heard counting, sometimes in correct sequence. One day while handling a small pile of stones, Nicky brought one to the bench where his mother was.

Placing the stone on the bench, he said, "This is *one*."

Then he went back to his pile of stones, picked up another one, and with fast steps brought it to the bench.

Placing this stone next to the first one, he looked at them and said louder than the first time, "And this is *two!*"

Apparently elated by his discovery, he ran back to the pile, picked up another single stone, and brought *it* to the bench.

Placing this stone with the other two, he recognized the changed quantity, exclaiming, "And this is *three!*"

Excitement of knowing *three* was unmistakable in Nicky's body and behavior. He ran to the pile of stones again, picked up one more stone, and rushed with it to the bench where he placed it alongside the others.

"And *this* is . . ." he started saying, hesitated a moment, and then concluded, "a lot."

It was the conclusion of his pursuit. Nicky did not go for an additional stone. He was sure of knowing *one*, *two*, and *three*. Also, he knew the limit of his mental effort and admitted it with-

*From: *Kindergarten: A Year of Learning* by Marguerita Rudolph and Dorothy H. Cohen. Copyright © 1964 by Meredith Publishing Company. By permission of Appleton-Century-Crofts, Educational Division, Meredith Corporation, pp. 313-314.

out losing face. His mother did not decide that he was *immature* because he did not know *four* and that she should supply him with this knowledge. She respected his wisdom of knowing his own limitation and the ingeniousness with which he terminated the lesson to himself.

From Nicky a teacher could learn to appreciate what the child truly *knows*, rather than measure what he does not know and prod him about it. Just as Nicky's knowledge of *three* does not mean he is ready for arithmetic, a child's attempt at writing does not mean he is ready for formal writing. He must have many opportunities for such attempts, explorations, and independent discoveries before he encounters more formal teaching if he is to bring experience to that situation later and if he is to enjoy some measure of success. Some preschoolers enjoy imaginative, pretend writing by doing *easy scribbling* that might resemble any language, right-to-left Hebraic or vertical Oriental. The process and product of scribbling give children the feel of a written page. Scribbling also occurs in play—putting up "signs," sending "letters," "writing stories." Such charming, highly individual, easy scribbling done on the child's own initiative promises to bring the original scribblers to the threshold of the difficult task of real writing later.

When a teacher makes markings on a child's productions and refers to the markings as *his* name, he is usually impressed and soon may try in his own way to write his name. Some four- and five-year-olds learn without being instructed to print the letters of their name. Others find the tasks of forming letters very strenuous and making the symbols in certain proximity to each other very difficult. Yet, writing their own name is important to some children, and they want to practice *and* practice until the self-imposed assignment is completed. It seems especially satisfying to older preschoolers to be able to write their own name on their drawings or paintings. The *name* sprawled over the paper sometimes has equal value with the painting or drawing itself; the letters of the name may be distributed in dominant positions and the rest of the space just filled in. Some preschool children do not try to write their name, though they want to see it written.

When Charles admired Jane's writing of her name, the teacher suggested that maybe he would like to try.

"No," responded Charles, seemingly quite sure of that. "You (meaning the teacher) can do it better!"

Charles preferred to have his name written "better."

Although the practice of writing the name is a beginning in writing, it is a temporary interest of the child under six, and its significance for him lies in the satisfaction of writing his own name. What this child now needs, therefore, is not more *writing*, but recognition for doing additional kinds of independently directed manual performance to enhance self-esteem. Such activities may include combing his hair before a mirror, distinguishing the right shoe from the left when putting them on, pouring a beverage, and serving his own food.

Through handling play and art materials children continually discover and compare *dimensions:* wide and narrow, short and long, straight and curve. For example, the children playing with strips of paper described earlier in this book were making use of length. When children select pieces from a collage collection and compose particular patterns, they have a chance to regard various dimensions and discover that a "small" piece by itself is "big" when compared with other pieces of the pattern. Cooking provides exciting encounters with dimension, too. Children notice the flat level of the batter in the pans and the full-risen volume of the baked product.

Young children in their own way can discern the tiniest of objects. Many toddlers pick up small scraps of matter barely visible to adults. Preschoolers, when their interest is aroused, show remarkable patience in arranging objects by size and comparing dimensions (not always with words) where size difference is a strong attribute.

Six pumpkins of different sizes were literally seized by a group of nursery school children, were measured by embraces, and were weighed by elaborate cooperative picking up. The absorption in discovering sizes was greater than the excitement of making jack-o'-lanterns!

"This is the biggest — my arms wouldn't go around it."

"This is the smallest — look, I can hold it with one hand!"

"Put the biggest one in the front."

Soon six pumpkins were being arranged by size, and the children encountered the problem of judging mathematical accuracy ("this one is a little tiny bit bigger"). Finding this problem in a natural, primitive way, muscularly and visually, did not mean they were ready for a sophisticated solution. So the teacher did not at that point introduce the use of a scale or ruler. Later, however, she did have in the room these familiar devices for measuring and weighing. The children then manipulated and experimented with these instruments, trying to understand the basic mechanics, while the teacher pointed out the reliability of the ruler and the balance scale.

There were similar responses to apples in another group. At snack time a teacher placed four apples on the cutting board in order of size. First, the children referred to them as "Daddy, Mommy, Brother, and Baby." This association was obviously made by concept of size. Then the children made various comments on bigness, smallness, and size differences. When the teacher proceeded to cut the apples in half, then quarters, then some quarters in half to make chunks, the children were interested not only in the diminishing sizes ("it's going to be littler"), but also in confronting a mathematical problem. Since each child wanted "a bigger piece" he tried to figure out which piece was bigger.

Further thinking about young children's handling of sizes and dimensions and discovering how objects fit makes it clear that some household utensils are excellent learning materials. Pots with their lids, for instance, are interesting not only to busy two-year-olds, but also to the more inquiring three-year-olds. Having the advantages of familiarity, manageability, and sound appeal, pots and lids are also useful for fascinating demonstrations of what a pot can contain, how content can disappear out of sight, concealed by a cover, and how perfectly a lid can *fit*. Measuring cups and spoons for play in a preschool are used more imaginatively than standard commercial nesting toys since they have real work association with home or school.

The meat grinder can be effectively employed as a learning material. It must be put together *correctly* to work and taken apart *completely* to clean. In handling it the children learn to finger the screws, turn the spiral part, and crank the long handle. The grinder has additional appeal for children by being a real working tool. To make it work requires concentration and coordination and invites a child to try again and again, as though the success filled him with energy.

When a child leaves the preschool full of energy and confidence and with experiences of success in working and learning, he will be an *advantaged* school child, equipped for learning important relevant skills.

14 Places to Go and People to Know

A preschool trip can be a touching sight for an outsider who observes a procession of small ones, single file or clutching hands two by two with hovering grown-ups—stepping into a rough, regulated world of busy streets, big doors, strange persons, and fascinating objects. The sight makes an observer turn around and look again at the lively faces of the small ones with the worried big ones nearby. The observer wants to follow them as they venture to a park where there is plenty of space for running or to a bakery where they are magnetically drawn to the window behind which are mounds of fresh buns.

Trips often disrupt routine and require tiresome but necessary arrangements with a particular place and decisions about what to take, whom to notify, and what additional supervision is needed. In spite of these factors, trips are not only loved by children, but also highly regarded by teachers, administrators, and parents. Trips spell educational opportunities, although for children they have the lure of adventure, a necessary ingredient in good preschool living. A trip does not necessarily mean going physically far or even away from the premises. Going to a new place to see "the world," to seek knowledge, and to have adventure may mean visiting a place very close to the preschool. It may mean also simply exploring the school itself and getting to know people at work in the building.

Although class trips should not be undertaken until the children become fully familiar with and secure in their own classroom and *ready* to venture out, there is a special visit that a teacher with a few children at a time can make quite early in the year. It is a visit to the school office. Each child might have been in the office before, accompanied by his mother or teacher. But a special visit planned with and for the children elicits different interest and more attention from them. They will enjoy looking at the secretary's desk, touching her supplies, and knowing where children's names and addresses are kept. Many will want to see the office machines in use. Here, then, will be an opportunity for the secretary to show what she does: typing, using the adding and duplicating machines, etc. She may receive or make a phone call and give a simple explanation about it. During one group's visit, a telephone message came in for the teacher who was not in the office. The secretary handed the written message to one of the children to deliver on the group's return to their room. The whole group was elated to bring a real message straight from the office.

During another group's visit, the time coincided with the secretary's coffee break so she shared a box of biscuits with the children as they proudly told her their names. The secretary, who knew the children's names on paper only, found the lively cluster of *real* children in her office to be a pleasant event! The visit lasted only 15 minutes, but the sociability between the secretary and the children lasted all year. Since a secretary and the office often serve as a connection between the home and the child's classroom, pleasant, meaningful encounters with the office help with good adjustment to school.

Another important section of a school building that interests young children (especially those living in apartments) is the basement. It usually has the heating system, the water pipes, a storage area, a repair shop perhaps, a tool place, other spots for special maintenance work, and most important a room or a place where the custodian keeps his belongings. The custodian, who keeps the school warm and clean for the children, is an important person to them!

Even though in one school the custodian worked evenings and the children did not see him, they were still interested in the special closet with his big mops and brooms, and they left him messages about repairs and thank you notes. One day the teacher and children invited him to come in for milk and cookies. He came and responded eagerly to their friendliness, and the feeling was reciprocal.

When young children see the custodian as they arrive at school, call him when anything breaks down, and see him cleaning up the place as they depart, they sometimes refer to *him* as "the boss of the school," for to them he takes care of their school in a more tangible way than a director. A teacher, therefore, should not take the custodian's work for granted, but should try to involve him educationally. For example, she and a few children may accompany him when a piece of outdoor equipment is being assembled, installed, or built and help him with raking or sweeping the yard. Children may also want to invite the custodian to some celebration.

A meaningful trip to be taken later in the year is to another classroom. The children may visit to get acquainted with next year's teacher, to use special play equipment in that class, to see an animal, or just to see what it is like in another class and become motivated to invite children for a reciprocal visit. Probably no more than two or three children can undertake such a visit, but it could still provide an important experience away from the classroom.

It can be concluded from the discussions of visits to the office and basement that a trip means not only a place to go, but also people to know. When a trip proves to be too difficult to arrange, it may be quite simple to plan for some important people to visit the children in their own classroom. Such important people may be grown-ups whose work relates directly to the children's well-being.

All preschool children are attracted to the garbage man, his big truck, and the large loads he lifts. They like to watch him perform his job and are ready to greet him as a person. On a day when the garbage collection takes place, the teacher and the children might leave the room to watch the garbage man at work. It is important for the teacher to find out whether he is called sanitation worker, refuse collector, or maybe even environmental protector so that the children may know his correct title. He may be able to come in for a few minutes if invited and answer questions about his work.

In one situation two garbage collectors emptied the trash baskets that the children had brought out and then accepted a child's offer of fruit juice. All the children watched the men drink the juice, and they talked about the event afterward. Another time they and the men waved to each other and exchanged greetings.

I have no illusions that *all* garbage men are kindly or even tolerant toward small children or toward teachers who want to involve workers. A teacher needs to be realistic about the particular workers on the premises and needs to find out what kind of people serve the preschool and with whom children can establish friendly contacts.

The milkman, making regular appearances at the preschool, may be willing to make slight changes in his route for a short visit. He may actually serve the children milk, and they may treat him with their cookies. He may sit at a table with them for a few minutes of informal conversation. Or, he might delight in having them inspect and get in the milk truck and even carry some milk containers.

Any adult worker is usually pleased with children's friendliness and genuine interest, as was the plumber described in an earlier chapter. Yet, some, whether they are menial workers or professional people, may find children's honesty in itself disconcerting.

When a nursery school teacher persuaded Dr. Bendick, a parent of a child in her class, to make a social call, he was uneasy, even apprehensive, in this strange role. It seemed as though he was worried about what the children might do to him if he was not in control. When a girl asked if he was a *real* doctor, he was not amused. The teacher then told the children Dr. Bendick *was* a real doctor and pointed to his doctor's bag. At that point he was willing to have them look at the contents in his bag. However, their poking fingers and their comments and questions seemed to bother him. Perhaps he felt the children in effect were *examining him*. It, therefore, seemed understandable that when some children invited him to see their woodworking room he shook his head; when they invited him for refreshments, he had no more time and zipped his bag. A little girl wanted to carry his bag but he said No with a smile.

Fortunately, there are many doctors who are able to shed their professional coats when visiting a preschool and enjoy seeing healthy, active, curious children.

"This is Dr. Bruce," the teacher said, introducing a visiting pediatrician.

"What's he going to do?" one child asked apprehensively.

The teacher assured the group that Dr. Bruce did not come to give shots or checkups.

"I came to see what children do in nursery school," he said.

"Why?" another child asked.

Dr. Bruce answered thoughtfully, "Because I don't know."

The children responded with eagerness and tried to attract his attention to all the equipment in the room. On parting, Dr. Bruce gave the children tongue depressors to add to their woodworking accessories. In that visit the children did not learn about the doctor's profession, but they learned about his interest in children as people, not as patients. Dr. Bruce was a well-remembered visitor.

Sometimes an exciting visitor can appear unexpectedly. Like an apparition, a delightful one to the children, a man with a moving sponge and pail rose full-length across the multipaned window.

"How is he holding on?"

"Is he going to wash all the windows in school?"

"He's lucky . . ."

"He's coming down now!"

When the window washer entered the classroom, he received not only a welcome, but also personal admiration that he never expected. Some children inspected his equipment. Others told him he was strong to wash so many windows, and a little girl asked if he had a little girl at home. The man smiled and held up two fingers. Most children left other activities and watched the window-washing operation.

An interesting visitor need not always be human. In fact an unforgettable day for all six classes in one preschool was the day when Josephine, the black goat, came. Every child was enchanted by the lively, greedy, stubborn, and surprisingly tame and friendly goat. The director had learned of Josephine's temporary stay in the neighborhood, and took advantage of it. The goat's visit was feasible since there was ample space in the school yard and the weather was congenial for both morning and afternoon children to be outside and become acquainted with Josephine. Feeding the goat bread was amusing, but having her snatch paper from the teacher's hand was hilarious! A dozen hands tentatively stretched to touch Josephine first. Then one child at a time, as suggested by the adult, touched the goat.

"It's hair . . . no, it's fur, fur! Feel it! That's her skin . . ."

The goat, tied to the fence by a long rope, moved fast as the children watched and admired her nimble feet. Suddenly Josephine was on top of the picnic table, starting to chew on a sweater! This obvious naughtiness at once endeared the goat to the children! They watched all the goat's movements and noticed all her features from the small tail to the big eyelashes. They observed her peculiar behavior from the indiscriminate munching of paper to the bleating that sounded like laughter to the children and caused them to imitate Josephine and roar with laughter.

"Will Josephine come again?" the children asked the goat's owner, for Josephine was a welcome, entertaining visitor who enlivened the day.

Visits in the immediate neighborhood can provide more interest and surprises for children than grown-ups would expect. When Blackie, the school rabbit, found his way under the fence into the next yard and inquiries were made, the results were mutual acquaintance with the next door neighbor: a visit—not through the fence but the front door—and a picnic in the neighbor's rose garden.

Through the fence in another area of the yard the children befriended a cat that belonged to a different neighbor and became acquainted with the neighbor and her family. Some people live for years without knowing who lives next door to them; this applies also to some preschools. Yet, just knowing who lives next door adds to social awareness and to friendliness in general.

A neighborhood may have some small shops, markets, or other businesses which would be especially worthwhile to visit. Interesting work and business transactions on a small scale are easier to see and consider and are more comprehensible to young children than are huge establishments. For example, with a few children a teacher might plan a trip to a small food store. The visit may be a valid class errand to purchase something needed such as cheese and crackers or berries and cream. Plans could entail finding out where supplies are stored, how cost is computed (by pencil from behind the ear, or by finger on a register), who the customers are, what the storekeeper says to customers, and what customers say.

Most urban neighborhoods and some suburban ones are likely to have a shoe repair shop with hand and machine operations, hammering and buzzing sounds, piles of worn shoes, shelves of fixed and tagged ones in rows, a discernable spicy leathery smell, and interesting, curious scraps. Small children who notice such things but who seldom have a chance to look, to touch, and to comment should have this opportunity. A real practical errand of bringing an adult's or child's shoes for repair makes the trip especially appealing and interesting. A follow-up trip to collect the repaired shoes offers still a different kind of interest and learning. Although only a few children in the group may get to see the work at the shop and get to know the workers by going on the trip, all the children in the class could see firsthand the shoes in both worn-out and repaired stages and have a chance to make creative use of discarded leather scraps collected at the shop.

If an auto service station is near, a carefully supervised visit is a must for any preschool group. Here, too, some personal experience makes the trip especially valuable for children. On one visit to a neighborhood service station a preschool group watched intently the gasoline *liquid* splash out of the hose. They had assumed until that time that gasoline transferred into the car was in a state of invisible *gas*. They noticed the underside of a hoisted automobile. They listened to the hissing sound of air going into a tire and imitated the sound. They were delighted with a gift of an inner tube from an interested attendant, who called the little boys "fellows." But the most impressive thing happened when they were ready to return to school. A blue car drove up to a gasoline pump and a familiar, smiling face greeted the children from behind the windshield of the car.

"Miss Fitchen!" the children called excitedly.

There was the school director, whose errand was real, but whose timing was planned.

"Did you come to get gas?"

"Did you know we came here, too?"

"Look what we got!"

Then the group watched with personal concern the director's car being filled with gasoline, the tires being puffed with air, and the windshield being wiped with a chamois cloth which one of the children wanted to touch. Then Miss Fitchen offered to take their cumbersome gift of the inner tube into the car and drove off.

When the children arrived at school on foot and saw the director's car, they recounted the pleasant surprise.

"You know what? When we went on a trip, Miss Fitchen came there!"

Although this trip was important for the practical information about cars and trucks which the children acquired, the surprise of meeting Miss Fitchen at the service station made the visit personal and memorable.

For children and adults a neighborhood trip around the block in which the school is located can be fascinating and fun as well as instructive, for pure geographic reasons and space orientation. One group of children and the teacher might go to the right and make only right turns; the remaining group might go to the left and make only left turns. Will they meet? At what point? When you leave and go in one direction, will you really come back from the other direction? What kind of buildings or structures do you pass going around the school? What would happen if you make a wrong turn? What landmarks tell you where you are? Real explorations! With interested teachers of older preschoolers such exploration can lead to map making, to giving directions on how to get to a place, and to describing a location. These are some fundamentals of travel, of space orientation, of awareness, of learning to understand location and position. Such powerful learning occurs from hand (but in this case from foot) to head.

To help assess the learning or the effect of any trip, the teacher joins in or initiates informal talk about it, observes dramatic play, and tries to present extra and new information from books and pictures in order to answer relevant questions. For example, on a trip to the grocery the children witnessed an annoyed housewife returning a loaf of moldy bread which the grocer kindly accepted and was going to put in the garbage. The teacher and children asked for the stale bread to feed their pet ducks. In the process they became interested in the mold and saved several pieces of bread. Daily they examined the bread and noticed the change in color, shape, and texture of the mold as it grew. The teacher, therefore, obtained a science picture book[1] (for older children) which she studied herself. Also, she showed the children pictures of molds and shared some concrete facts, new and interesting to her. She would not have learned about the value and beauty of living molds if it had not been for the children's curiosity which was aroused spontaneously as an incidental part of the trip.

Many teachers find a trip to a small bakery to be a favorite of

[1] Bernice Kohn. *Our Tiny Servants: Molds and Yeasts,* illustrated by John Kaufmann. Englewood Cliffs, N. J.: Pentice-Hall, Inc., 1962.

preschool children. The familiarity of many of the goods as well as the previous knowledge of the basic bakery ingredients (salt, shortening, sugar, flour) helps make the meaning of what is going on in a bakery understandable. The big barrel and bowls, the stirring apparatus, the marvelous malleable dough, and, of course, the men at work make the trip to a bakery a "great" experience. Then there is the real, appetizing attraction of freshly baked goodies with tantalizing aromas for children to sample and to take home! If the trip is easy to arrange, it is worth repeating at a later time.

Trips to see construction and demolition activities, street repairs in a city neighborhood, and harvesting in a rural neighborhood are among many other meaningful trips too numerous to include in one book. But for the final example of a trip, the focus is on one especially impressive to all young children. This is a trip to the teacher's home, assuming the distance does not make such a trip impossible. Little children appear to be unable to separate the teacher from the preschool where they know her; they cannot picture her as ever being anywhere else. Thus, to be able to actually step into the teacher's other home (to them her home essentially is where they know her) is a revelation!

"Do you have a real bed?" Then the bed is tested for reality. The bathroom, too, is promptly tried out by practically every child.

"Where do you cook?" A kitchen is a very important part of a home and another proof that the teacher's home is "real." Other items of daily living are inspected and checked with great interest.

Food on the teacher's table seems especially appetizing, and eating in her house adds to children's sense of relation to the teacher. Altogether the visit serves in a most personal way to expand their concept of knowing another person.

15 Striving for Concepts in Preschool Education

A four-year-old may say "We are going on a picnic Friday," but he has no concept of the passing of time and the days before Friday. "Is today Friday?" he asks every day. *Friday* is merely a word of designation. He arrives at a concept of time at a slow, complicated pace after many experiences. What *is* a concept in a pure practical sense? Perhaps a definition will evolve from a discussion of what a concept is *not* and from a review of accounts of real classroom incidents presented in previous chapters.

A concept is not expressed in memorized talk, such as reciting the alphabet in sequence (even singing it) or saying a telephone number correctly, although such information is sometimes needed and is always impressive for adults to hear. A concept is not having factual information, useful as it may be, such as you need a shovel to dig, the broom belongs in the closet, or you need to have money to get ice cream from the jingling truck.

Nicky was using and in his way studying one stone then another, then a third, saying in conclusion "and this is three." Thus, he was revealing his concept of *three*, his comprehension that evolved from experience and that was expressed in behavior and words.

Children explored the concept of size as they themselves arranged pumpkins in relation to size and as they worked in fitting measuring cups one inside the other. Concepts of shape and dimension as well as color were involved in their selecting and attaching collage materials. Children became aware of the concept of change as it occurred in their cooking experience when they saw changes of color, of consistency of food, and of physical state as when perceivable sugar dissolved and became invisible. Children may understand other concepts of the physical world such as the concept of weight experienced by filling, lifting, and holding a bag of sand.

Children's concepts of the social world are more complicated to demonstrate. However, the accounts which follow may help the reader understand how children in preschool express social concepts.

In an urban child care center two friends were enjoying each other's company. Walter had fair skin and light hair; Conrad had dark skin and black hair. They were walking slowly up two long flights of steps to their room, and in typical four-year-old fashion they noticed the details of their raincoats. The teacher behind them eavesdropped on the conversation.

"Mine has shiny buttons."

"And mine has hooks." They mentioned other details as well as the different colors.

"You know what?" Walter suggested in the middle of their leisurely sociability, at the first landing. "Let's change our raincoats — and then they won't know who we are." . . .

"Yea, let's," Conrad agreed. They both giggled excitedly at the prospect of not being recognized by their friends.

"They'll think I am you!" Conrad qualified with complete naiveté.

"And they'll say I am Conrad," Walter added. The two children laughed congenially, in anticipation of mystifying their mates with the transformation. As the teacher helped with the exchange of raincoats, she realized that this belief in transformation by means of clothing was characteristic of children's play. She was curious, though, about the boys' scheme, and was eager to hear more.

"But they might find out," one suddenly said.

"So we'll keep each other's raincoats on — so they can't tell."

"But maybe they could . . ."

"How?" Their pace slackened as they stopped playing and speculated how their true identity might be revealed in spite of a concealing attire. The teacher walking behind them listened.

"*Maybe*—they could tell by our voices," one child said, thinking apparently of a distinctive personal difference. Voice indeed distinguishes more profoundly the unique identity of a person than does skin color or racial features or clothing.*

Thus the four-year-olds revealed their thinking and judgment in expressing a concept of distinguishing characteristics of individual persons. This was a social—psychological concept arrived at in the process of a congenial relationship, just two friends, *left alone*, to think and talk by themselves.

A young child who is first mostly concerned with and aware of himself gains gradually a concept of other people from daily personal experiences in the preschool group. The little girl who was concerned with getting enough cherries for herself became *first* aware of the threatening appetites of others. Later, with her own needs satisfied, she responded to the enticing activities of other children and felt pleasure at being in their midst.

The child's preschool experiences with other children as well as with adults are of course not all sweetness, friendliness, and accommodation to him. Conflicts, quarrels, and hurts of many kinds occur during his living and struggling with, relating to, and testing other children in preschool. If these encounters are infrequent and of short duration, a child lives through them, matures in the process, and gains concepts of *other* children.

A young child knows adults mostly in the intimate circle of his own family. In preschool he has experience with grown-ups *other* than family members. He has continuing contact with his teachers. He receives occasional greetings from other school adults, talks to the custodian when he sees him, notices friendly visitors, and experiences "breaking bread" as he eats with others. Continued natural exposure to and meaningful personal encounters with grown-ups enable a child to form a concept of adults.

Lack of response or some misunderstanding may temporarily thwart a teacher-child relationship. With goodwill and trust on the part of adults, the relationship can be repaired. As a result, a child grows and reaches for understanding. This concept of other people is naturally affected by all of the child's social experiences: by what he finds he has in common, by demonstration of differences, by challenges from others.

A young child has a sense of security and identification with

*From *Living and Learning in Nursery School* by Marguerita Rudolph. New York: Harper & Row, Publishers, 1954, pp. 64-65.

grown-ups in his life. A significant attribute of "grown-upness" is work, "real" work as children themselves say. There is a current concern in both government and education about the concept and reality of work in our society. One result of official studies indicates that a troublesome number of adults and youths do not value work and show serious lack of aptitudes. To combat this in New York State, the Board of Regents issued (June 1971) a proposal in a seventeen-page position paper. According to this proposal, "children in elementary schools would develop an appreciation of *the value of work and the worker* and an awareness of their own aptitudes in relation to various occupations." Elementary school includes *young children* five to eight years of age. Therefore, concern with concepts of work and workers in preschool is relevant in the light of current social needs.

In the previous chapter the appeal that real life has for young children and their interest in understanding work and workers were emphasized. Exchanging greetings with the window washer, touching his work equipment, and seeing the bright results of his work left the child with a positive image. Meeting the man with his garbage truck, picking up a trash basket, and sharing refreshment with the workman enabled the child to feel on common, human ground with the workman.

Having a uniformed traffic policeman or fireman actually in the children's midst on an informal visit as well as seeing him at work gives children and teachers a humanized view of traffic conducting, fire fighting, etc., and personal interest in preventing trouble. Seeing the shoemaker, tailor, or baker *at work* using his special skill, producing something unquestionably useful and even praiseworthy, helps children understand the work and *feel* what it is like to be a worker. Such *personal experiences* coupled with the young child's natural power of imagination and his capacity to play build his concept of work. Watch his concentration in "driving a bus," with full attention to the "vehicle" and the "passengers." Observe the patience of the "waiter" taking orders in a "restaurant." Listen to the chant and notice the persuasive manner of the "balloon salesman."

Children's responsiveness to concepts of work and workers needs to be recognized and further nurtured by adults. What then is the teacher's responsibility and how can her influence be assessed? What are the teacher's own attitudes and thinking about work and workers?

An educationally qualified director of an established middle-class *white* nursery school and kindergarten was discussing her program and standards with a consultant. Both the director and consultant were satisfied with the preschool's accredited staff, properly filled out health forms, purchase of recommended equipment, and other routine aspects of the program. Then the consultant brought up the question of the school's status of racial integration. How did the director feel about the school being in a community having non-white residents but serving only white children. The director professed her "fondest desire" to enroll non-white children, but quickly commented that the parents just were not applying, probably because of the fee. She noted further that only the Board, not she, decided on scholarships. Then the consultant wanted to know if there was anything compensatory which the director was doing to bring the enrolled children in contact with non-white people.

"Why, yes!" the director proudly said. "The man who is in the building a good deal and whom the children see practically every day and like—the janitor—is a black man."

"And do the children know him?" queried the consultant.

"They should," came the reply, "for I made a point *to explain* to the children what Ben, the Janitor, does: how he attends to *all* the sweeping and *all* the scrubbing in the whole two-story building, how he comes in very early in the morning and how *hard* he works, and how all of us should appreciate hard-working Ben."

"Were there any comments from the children that might show what this explanation meant to them?" the consultant asked.

"Why, yes," said the director, "they listened attentively and they talked about Ben."

The director commented further that she was really *amused* by Randy's question: "Did Ben's skin get dark because he worked so hard?"

So this is Randy's concept of work, influenced by an adult's attitude and words: *Work is extreme menial servitude; and the people whose lot it is to engage in work turn black from exertion!*

Actually Randy did not *know* the worker. Randy had only a glimpse of him in passing and noted his distinguishing blackness. Randy never had an opportunity to notice anything else because he was never in on Ben's work and never talked to him personally. The director, with her authority, provided only a description of the worker in benevolent, pitying terms.

What then was the director's value of work and workers? Perhaps Randy's concept of work reflected not only the director's values, but also those of the predominantly white community in which there was lack of contact with and lack of knowledge of non-white people working in many different occupations. Could not such ignorance be remedied by realistic experience and discussion?

Teachers as practicing members of a democratic society must feel and demonstrate respect for all groups of useful workers in order to effectively provide children who are at a young, impressionable age with experiences that build positive attitudes toward concepts of work. In doing this, there are some *attributes* of work experience which are important to children as they begin to know work themselves.

It is important for a child to have *pride* and pleasure *in his own prowess*, whether carrying a chair, moving a table, using hand muscles effectively to extract orange juice, or knowing where to go and what to say in delivering a message. Also it is good for a child to sense the importance of *doing many things for himself* (simple as those things may seem to adults): pouring his own drink in spite of spills, folding his own cot or blanket even if it takes a struggle, fastening his own jacket even if it comes out wrong and undoing it and fastening again, taking part in cleaning his room or scrubbing his table (of course, done with some playing on the side). Here teachers should note that the adult notion of sex differences in children's activities has clearly outlived its usefulness and effectiveness. In today's society it is as important for little boys' sense of *self-sufficiency* to do domestic chores as it is for little girls' sense of *independence* to develop manual, mechanical, and muscular skills in the course of daily living. Self-sufficiency and independence are of equal value to girls' and boys' development in the preschool years.

Children experience considerable satisfaction when they are able to share the results of their labor. This happens when flowers from planted seeds are admired and a bouquet is enjoyed by the class, when harvested radishes are actually eaten by the children and grown-ups, when the pan of corn bread the group baked is large enough for each child to take a piece home to mother.

An even more complicated concept, but one that directly and indirectly enters children's awareness and learning, is the concept of environment. Teachers must look at environment in the bright light of present knowledge of the vulnerable and wounded planet Earth. Then, after seeing children's responses, activities, personal interests, imagination, and inventiveness, the teacher can plan to engage children in knowing, using, and caring to protect the environment in the course of basic preschool education. A first consideration should be knowing the immediate environment through personal contact and pleasurable experience, thus sharpening and deepening both children's and teachers' awareness.

A second consideration should be the adults' understanding of the universal concern for the ongoing environmental destruction which comes with advancement and progress. How much understanding is there of continued spoilage, pollution, and destruction of the natural resources of the Earth? The total extent, the scope, and the intricate technical and economic causes of environmental destruction are beyond young children's conception, but specific manifestations and demonstrable destruction are not overlooked by children. Closing of a nearby beach by health authorities is a relevant topic for discussion by young children, with the teacher supplying basic facts on the nature and great danger of pollution.

Specific relevant information on pollution that teachers share with the children can elicit constructive concern. There are many national, regional, and state organizations which can provide recent statistical, pictorial, and social facts and figures. Local newspapers are useful resources, too, since they generally feature immediate environmental disasters as well as programs geared to recycling, reclamation, etc.

There is graphic demonstration of un-buryable, un-burnable refuse of different kinds that children can see somewhere near in any community. They can also see evidence of pollution in any body of water, little or big. *Where* does it come from? From too much! Too much use of electricity—some people have *electric* shoeshine brushes! Too much automobile driving—many people have more than one car! Too much paper production—paper bags and paper boxes and wrappings to unwrap and throw away! *Who*, who pollutes? People? You? Me?

What can teachers and preschoolers do then? They can be their own *waste watchers*! What is in the wastebasket? What was thrown away in one morning? in one day? Make a list. Take a count. A hundred and eleven pieces of paper! No, probably more! Were the crumpled paper towels counted? Yes, some paper towels in there are still clean! The other side of those thrown-away drawing papers could be used for another activity. Then there would not be so much in the wastebasket. Look at the three milk cartons sticking up. They take up lots of room. Squash them then; squash the cartons flat. Why is that big juice can taking up room? Could it be stepped on and squashed? Anybody can do that! Yes, old metal *is* good for something. Factories make *new* metal out of it. So, why not collect from school and from home a big bunch of flat, squashed metal cans and take them to a recycling station.

Thus from experience a *concept of usefulness of waste* can be developed in children, provided, of course, that adults are free of the American addiction to reckless waste production and of living a disposable throwaway life. If adults are addicted, then a change of values is needed for sheer survival. The obvious value of economizing and conserving which has bearing on reducing waste and preserving the essentials *is* within the mental grasp of young children.

During a year of severe drought when use of water had to be officially curtailed, the nursery school children knew what it meant to use only a little water and to avoid wasting. They understood that when the use of water was limited the small available amount would last longer. Children turned the faucets on with great care, saved waste water for plants, and rationed water outdoors for an improvised kind of hand washing. One child poured a small amount of water into a pair of cupped hands for scrubbing and then a rationed amount for rinsing.

Young children can learn to be economical and to develop a concept of saving the environment probably quicker than adults. In such learning that proceeds from hand to head, perhaps young children can help us appreciate the simple and the natural. Perhaps they can inspire us to greater, more honest efforts to achieve good living on planet Earth.

In writing this last chapter my chief concern has been the human problems of living together with respect between generations and peoples and of caring sensibly about the environment where living takes place. Therefore, considerable attention was given to concepts of work and people and to the urgent need for ecological knowledge in the hope that positive concepts in those areas can be gained in the early years when *active* learning is part of the growing child.

Bibliography

Professional Books

All references relate to studying, guiding, and learning from children. A few booklets and pamphlets are included.

Biber, Barbara. *Premature Structuring as a Deterrent to Creativity.* New York: Bank Street College of Education Publications, 1958. This pamphlet elucidates the hazards of early structuring of learning and points to the teacher's delicate role in the dynamics of creative involvement of children.

Dittman, Laura D., ed. *Curriculum Is What Happens.* Washington, D.C.: National Association for the Education of Young Children, 1970. Outstanding educational specialists present different kinds of new preschool programs and discuss ways of augmenting established programs.

Encyclopaedia Britannica, Inc. *The Young Children's Encyclopaedia.* 16 vol. Chicago: Encyclopaedia Britannica, Inc., 1971. This set is especially geared to attract, inform, and interest young children. It has sensible organization of subjects, easy-to-use references, appealing format, manageable volume size, and quality art work. There is an accompanying Parent's Manual.

Fraiberg, Selma H. *The Magic Years: Understanding and Handling the Problems of Early Childhood.* New York: Charles Scribner's Sons, 1959. A chronological presentation of happenings in the human life of the child, as well as the author's literary style, makes this a helpful and happy book, rich and original in the insight it offers.

Furth, Hans G. *Piaget for Teachers.* Englewood Cliffs, N.J.: Prentice-Hall, Inc., 1970. Piaget's theories of intellectual development, as a basis for understanding the need to nurture intelligence in children, are clarified. The author discusses school situations that stimulate thinking, and points out that it is thinking not rote learning that matters in education.

Ginott, Haim G. *Between Parent and Child.* New York: The Macmillan Co., 1965. A psychotherapist, agressively on the child's side, gives impressive demonstrations of meaningful discipline, praise, and criticism, and of other areas of parent-child relationships.

Griffin, Louise. *Books in Preschool: A Guide to Selecting, Purchasing, and Using Children's Books.* Washington, D.C.: National Association for the Education of Young Children, 1971. This unusual reference deals with many areas of experience and suggests books about and for different ethnic groups.

Isaacs, Susan. *The Nursery Years: The Mind of the Child From Birth to Six Years.* New York: Schocken Books, Inc., 1968. In offering sound advice on managing children, the author places emphasis on answering their questions.

Montessori, Maria. *The Absorbent Mind.* New York: Holt, Rinehart & Winston, Inc., 1967 (Adyar, Madras, India: The Theosophical Publishing House, 1963). Maria Montessori reveals the absorbent, rather than merely receptive, mind of the young child. She shows great admiration for the child's physical and mental energies and his astonishing capacities for learning, in spite of obstacles and without the guidance of teachers. A cogent chapter is "Intelligence and the Hand."

Pratt, Caroline. *I Learn from Children: An Adventure in Progressive Education.* New York: Simon & Schuster, Inc., 1948. This is a challenging autobiography of a creative educator who a half century ago founded and guided an experimental school where children learned from their own experiences.

Shuey, Rebekah M., et. al. *Learning About Children.* Philadelphia: J. B. Lippincott Co., 1969, 3rd ed. Addressed to high school and junior college students, as well as to baby-sitters, this book extensively and practically covers early education, with reference to children in other countries.

Sunderlin, Sylvia, assoc. ed. *Bits and Pieces: Imaginative Uses for Children's Learning.* Washington, D.C.: Association for Childhood Education International, 1967. Early childhood practitioners write about a wide range of classroom activities, notably science.

Wylie, Joanne, co-ord. ed. *A Creative Guide for Preschool Teachers: Goals, Activities, and Suggested Materials for an Organized Program.* Racine, Wis.: Western Publishing Co., Inc., 1965. Large photographs and suggested professional and children's books add to the usefulness of this guide.

Adult Fiction

These few works that throw psychological light on the essence of childhood are suggested to encourage the reader to review and search for other artistic literature with similar emphasis.

Child Study Association of America. *A Reader for Parents: A Selection of Creative Literature About Children.* New York: W. W. Norton & Co., Inc., 1963. Included in this collection that covers a range of worldwide childhood experiences are short stories, poems, and excerpts from stories, novels, and autobiographies by Shakespeare, Tolstoy, Updike, and others.

O'Conner, Frank. *The Stories of Frank O'Conner.* New York: Alfred A. Knopf, Inc., 1952. Several stories in this collection deal with young children of poor Irish families and are written with earthy strength and humor.

Porter, Katherine Anne. *The Leaning Tower and Other Stories.* New York: Harcourt Brace Jovanovich, Inc., 1944. (Now available from Dell in paperback.) One of these realistic stories, "The Downward Path to Wisdom," shows the meaning of the different names by which a child is called.

Saroyan, William. *Little Children.* London: Faber & Faber, Ltd., 1937. Each short story is written with artistic simplicity that conveys observations and feelings for small details in a child's life. "The First Day of School," especially memorable, causes the reader to share the dilemmas and unique delights of a small child.

Children's Books

This small sample of titles, old and new, include some artistic books that young children like to have and to hold, some that provide pure enjoyment, and some books that elicit loud laughter.

Bronin, Andrew. *Behind the Wheel.* Illustrated by the author. New York: Holt, Rinehart & Winston, Inc., 1972. This fascinating paperback edition about all kinds of transportation is of interest to a child of any age.

Clark, Margery. *Poppy Seed Cakes.* Illustrated by Maud and Miska Petersham. New York: Doubleday & Co., Inc., 1929. A boy from "the old country," whose innocent mischief leads him to fantastic encounters, is the central character in this collection of stories.

Dobrin, Arnold. *Gerbils.* New York: Lothrop, Lee & Shepard Co., Inc., 1970. A book for teachers to read and adapt for young children. It contains information on the nature, behavior, and care of gerbils and has very good illustrations by the author.

Ets, Marie H. *Gilberto and the Wind.* New York: The Viking Press, Inc., 1963. A child discovers the immense range of the wind's dramatic action.

Gabel, Margaret. *Sparrows Don't Drop Candy Wrappers.* Illustrated by Susan Perl. New York: Dodd, Mead & Co., 1971. The do's and don'ts for dealing with pollution are easy to translate for young children. Graphic and amusing pictures add to their understanding.

Grover, Eulalie Osgood, ed. *Mother Goose: The Classic Volland Edition.* Illustrated by Frederick Richardson. Northbrook, Ill.: Hubbard Press, 1971. Here is a true children's classic with appealing nonsense and with poetry to evoke laughter, action, and song.

Krauss, Ruth. *The Carrot Seed.* Illustrated by Crockett Johnson. New York: Harper & Row, Publishers, 1945. A small boy encounters discouragements from everyone, but his perseverance and faith make him a winner.

Lionni, Leo. *Little Blue and Little Yellow.* Stamford, Conn.: Astor-Honor, Inc., 1959. A surprising book that represents friends and families with only colored abstract shapes for the illustrations.

Miles, Betty. *Mr. Turtle's Mystery.* Illustrated by Jacqueline Tomes. New York: Alfred A. Knopf, Inc., 1961. The disappearance of a small pet, the search through the house, and the reappearance of the turtle are absorbing and mysterious.

Minarik, Else Holmelund. *Little Bear.* Illustrated by Maurice Sendak. New York: Harper & Row, Publishers, 1961. The beauty of this very human story (in the guise of bears) lies in its harmony of text and pictures, creating a perfect blend of fantasy and reality.

Mitchell, Lucy Sprague, and Irma S. Black, eds. *Believe and Make-Believe.* Illustrated by Ayola Gordon. New York: E. P. Dutton & Co., Inc., 1956. Humorous verses, fantasy tales, and stories of the physical world by twenty-five authors are contained in this anthology.

Rudolph, Marguerita. *I Like a Whole One.* Illustrated by John E. Johnson. New York: McGraw-Hill Book Co., 1968. Arthur, the hero, does not meet with family approval when he prefers a whole apple, an uncut banana, and a complete pear. But he works out a solution and wins approval.

Selsam, Millicent E. *Seeds and More Seeds: A Science I Can Read Book.* Illustrated by Tomi Ungerer. New York: Harper & Row, Publishers, 1959. This book has many questions from a child's point of view, information that elicits wonder, and a story which is of equal interest to children and adults.

Tashjian, Virginia A. *Juba This and Juba That: Story Hour Stretches for Large or Small Groups.* Illustrated by Victoria de Larrea. Boston: Little, Brown & Co., 1969. The rhyming games, folk chants, riddles, stories for audience participation, musical plays, and more allow for improvisation by children or storyteller.

Index

Accident, to child, 115–116
  (see also Safety)
Animals, 19–31
  care of, 26
  death of, 27–29
  mating of, 29–31
  objections to, 20–21, 25
  source of learning, 20, 31
  spontaneous encounters with, 22–23
  suitable for classroom, 21–22
  teacher's responsibility for, 26
  visits by, 24–25, 136–137
  visits to, 21, 23, 24–25
Art media:
  blocks, 81, 82, 93–94
  buttons, 95
  chalk, 91
  clay, 80–81, 91
  collage, 92–93
  criteria for, 83, 85, 86, 91
  for dancing, 86
  household items as, 95–96
  how to choose, 90–93
  industrial materials, leftover, 96
  mud, 101–102
  musical instruments as, 85–86
  paints, 89, 90, 91–92
  pipe cleaners, 91
  play dough, 91
  puppets, 85
  purpose, as criterion, 91
  records, 83
  sand, 100–101
  seeds, 105, 106
  snow, 82
  special paper, 96
  spools, 96
  sticks, 104–105
  stones, 102
  wood, 93

Birthday celebration, child's, 112–113
  planning, 113
  props for, 113
  teacher's role in, 113
  (see also Celebrations; Holidays)
Blocks (block building), 81–82, 93–94,
      124–125
Body parts:
  learning function of, 7–8
  learning names of, 6–7
Books, 7, 28n, 30, 31n, 41n, 75n, 83n,
      88n, 94n, 98, 102n, 115n, 128n,
      139, 143n
  place in preschool room, 123

Celebrations:
  birthday, child's, 112–113
  centennial, 111–112
  international, 111
  as learning experience, 111–112
  national, 111
  regional, 111

Celebrations – Continued
  special weeks, 112
  teacher's role in, 111, 113
  (see also Birthday celebration; Holi-
      days)
Child, 6–11, 146
  himself, 6–11
  as multimedia artist, 80–96
  possessions, important to, 10–11
Christmas tree, 111
Class trips, 132–140
  to animals, 24–25
  to another classroom, 134
  around the block, 139
  arrangements for, 132
  to beach, 100
  to construction site, 140
  educational opportunities, 132–133
  in neighborhood, 137–139
  to rural area, 140
  to school basement, 133–134
  to school office, 133
  to service station, 138–139
  to shoe repair shop, 137–138
  to small bakery, 139–140
  to teacher's home, 140
  teacher's role in, 135, 139
  train, 65
  (see also Visits)
Clay, 80–81
Cloth scraps, 95–96
Collage construction, 92–93
Collections, 95–96, 102–106
  (see also specific entries)
Community events:
  as learning experience, 119
  strike, 119
  teacher's role in, 119–120
Concepts (see Preschool, concepts in)
Cooking, 42–53
  advanced, 51–52
  adventure in, 50
  encounters with change, 45–46
  encounters with time, 45
  language development in, 44
  as learning experience, 43–44
  mathematics development in, 44–45
  objections to, 42
  objectives of, 43
  place in curriculum, 52
  planning for, 50–51
  as sensory experience, 42–53
  teacher's responsibilities in, 42–43, 48,
      50, 53
  what to prepare, 46–48, 49, 51, 52, 53

Death of child, 116–118
  discussion of, in classroom, 117–118
  parents' attitude toward, 117–118
  teacher's role in, 116–118
Death of classroom animal, 27–29
Dramatic family play, 17, 18, 139
Dramatic pretending, 81

Eating:
  as learning experience, 32–41
  teacher, with children, 40

Family:
  attitude toward death, 117–118
  and birthday celebration, 113
  and cooking projects, 46, 52
  dramatic play, 17
  as educational resource, 16, 38, 68
  and home atmosphere, 12–18
  visit, by member of, 14–16
  visit to, 16–17
Family, child's, 12–18
Feathers, 105
Fire drill, 76
Fire safety, 72–77
  candles, lighting of, 73
  cooking, 73
  group discussion of, 76
  open fire, making, 73–75
  pain, as conditioning factor, 73
  role of classroom activities, 73
  teacher's role in, 71, 72, 73, 76
  visit to firehouse, 76–77
Food, as learning experience, 32–41
Foods in classroom:
  beans, 36
  cottage cheese, 37–38
  eggs, 34–36
  ethnic, 39, 109–110
  fruit juice, 36–37
  holiday, 109–110
  as nutrition lesson, 40–41

Games, for sensory experience, 8–9

Happenings, unexpected:
  accident, to child, 115–116
  assassination, 119–120
  community events, 119
  death of child, 116–118
  disasters, 118–119
  as learning experience, 114–115
  school vandalism, 114–115
Holidays, 107–111
  Christmas, 110–111
  ethnic traditions, 110–111
  as learning experience, 107, 109, 111
  Lincoln's birthday, 84, 109
  Martin Luther King's birthday,
    109
  Thanksgiving, 107–108
  Washington's birthday, 109
  (see also Celebrations)
Home atmosphere, 12–18
  affect on child, 12–13
  importance to teacher, 12, 13, 18
  sources of information about, 13
Household materials (utensils):
  as art media, 95–96
  as learning materials, 131
Housekeeping area, 17–18
  equipment, 17
  props for, 17, 18
  teacher's responsibility for, 17–18

Literacy, threshold of, 121–131

Mud (mud play), value of, 101–102
Multimedia artist, child as, 80–96
Music, 84, 85, 111
  as art experience, 85–86
"Musical" instruments, to make, list,
    86–87

Natural materials, 97–106
  dirt, 97
  feathers, 105
  mud, 101–102
  sand, 100–101
  seashells, 104
  seeds, 105–106
  snow, 99–100
  sticks, 104–105
  stones, 102–104
  water, 97–99
Nutrition lesson, 40–41

Occasions, special, 107–120
  (see also Celebrations; Holidays)

Painting, 87–90
  teacher's criticism of, 90
Parent(s), 13, 18, 52, 70, 96, 100
  cooperative, 1, 15
  (see also Family)
Pegboards, 123–124
People, to know, 132–140
Performing arts, 83, 85–87
  props for, 86–87
Personal powers, learning about, 9–10
Pipe cleaners, 91
Places, to visit, 132–140
  (see also Class trips; Visits)
Plant laboratory, in classroom, 57–58
Planting project, 57–58
Plants, 54–60
  acorns, 55
  in immediate environment, 56
  as learning experience, 54, 56, 59
  milkweed, 54
  outside of classroom, 60
  potatoes, 55–56
  project, planting, 57–58
  seeds, 55
  "sickness" of, 59
  as source of fuel, 57
  as source of nourishment, 56
  teacher's role in, 55, 56, 58
  trees, 55, 57
  usefulness of, 56–57
Possessions, importance, to child, 10–11
Preschool:
  cooking, in curriculum, 42–43, 52
  materials for, 123–125
    (see also specific entries)
  parents, concern for, 70
  purpose, 121
  school behavior emphasized, 122
  silent symbols, use of, 121–122
  teacher's role in, 122–123, 128
  vs. traditional school, 121
Preschool, concepts in, 141–148
  of adults, 143
  of color, 142
  defined, 141

153

Preschool, concepts in—*Continued*
  of environment, 146–148
  of other children, 143
  of other people, 143
  of shape, 142
  of size, 142
  social, 142–143
  teacher's role in, 144–145, 146, 147
  of work and workers, 144–146
Preschool program, 128
  reading in, 122
  safety in, 71
  writing, place of, in, 122, 129–130
Preschool teacher, assets, 1–5
  (*see also* Teacher; Teacher's responsi-
    bilities; Teacher's role)
Projects, special:
  cooking, 46–48, 51–52
  planting, 57–58
  nutrition, 40–41
  rock collection, 103–104
  tasting, 37–38
Props:
  for birthday celebration, 113
  for housekeeping area, 17–18
  for performing arts, 86–87
  for transportation play, 66–67
Puppets, 85
Puzzles, 123

Recognition, on job, 1, 5
Rocks (*see* Projects, special; Stones)
Role playing, 83–84

Safety, 70–79
  accidents, frequency, time of, 78
  affect of fear on, 71, 72
  common areas of, 71–75, 77–79
  fire, 72–77
  indoors, 79
  inspection, of equipment, 77–78
  large outdoor equipment, 77–79
  as learning experience, 70
  rules, 78–79
  stationary swing and, 79
  teacher's responsibility in, 66, 70, 78–
    79, 96
  tire swing and, 79
  traffic, 72
Sand (sand play), 100–101
Seashells, 105–106
Seeds, 105–106
  poisonous, warning about, 18, 55, 106
Sharing, difficult for child, 11
Snow, as art medium, 82
Snow (snow play), 99–100
Snow sculpture, 100
Snow stepping, 97
Stones, 102–104
  teacher supervision, need for, 104

Tasks, for young child, 10–11
Tasting lesson, 37–38
Teacher:
  as art critic, 87, 88, 89, 90
  attitude toward children, 3–4
  as botanist, 55, 58, 60
  eating, with children, 40

Teacher—*Continued*
  as human being, 1–5
  and self-examination, 32
Teacher's assistant (aide), 2, 3, 15, 39,
    50–51, 52, 89, 91
  mother, 110
Teacher's responsibilities:
  for classroom animals, 26
  in cooking, 42–43, 48, 50, 53
  in housekeeping area, 17–18
  in performing arts, 85–86
  in safety procedures, 70, 78–79, 96
Teacher's role:
  in accident to child, 115–116
  in birthday celebration, 113
  in celebrations, 111, 113
  in class trips, 135, 139
  in community events, using, 119–120
  in death of child, 116–118
  in fire safety, 71, 72, 73, 76
  in nature projects, 55, 56, 58, 59
  in preschool, 122–123, 128
  in preschool concepts, 144–145, 146,
    147
  in sand play, 101
  in snow play, 99–100
  in transportation, 62–63
  in vandalism to school, 114–115
Traffic safety, 72
  (*see also* Safety)
Transportation, 61–69
  aid in learning direction, 62
  construction of vehicles, 67–68
  direct experience with, 66
  interest, in people of, 64–65
  interest, in vehicles, 61, 62, 63–64
  as learning experience, 61–69
  means to enlarge power concept, 63
  in nature, 68–69
  picture sources for, 67
  planned experiences in, 68
  play experiences, 66–67
  props for, 66–67
  realistic pictures, aid in, 67
  role of energy in, 63
  teacher's guidance in, 62–63
  teacher's respect for safety in, 66
Travel, interest in, 62, 64
Trips (*see* Class trips)

Vandalism, to school, 114–115
Visits:
  to animals, 21, 23, 24–25
  of animals, to school, 24–25, 136–137
  to family, 16–17
  by family member, 14–16
  to firehouse, 76–77
  in immediate neighborhood, 137
  (*see also* Class trips)
Visits, of outside people, 3, 134–136
  doctor, 135–136
  garbage collector, 134–135
  milkman, 135
  traffic policeman, 64
  window washer, 136

Water (water play), 97–99
Woodworking, 93